**WILL SHAKESPE**

*The Comical, Tragical History of* WILLIAM
SHAKESPEARE (*with an Account of his
Conquests and Passions, Jealousies and Hatreds,
Struggles and Successes*), *as narrated by Jack
Rice, one time Boy Actor in Shakespeare's
Company.*

With diverse Supporting Roles played by his
Wife, Mistress Anne Hathaway; that ranting King
of Actors, Dick Burbage; the Dark lady with her
wanton wiles, who did play no small part in
Shakespeare's Sonnets – and in his Lusts; My
Fine Lord Southampton, who tempted Will to
silken sheets and sinful pleasures, but inspired
much Poetry-Making. And the Great Globe itself,
whose 'Wooden O' did see enacted such Drama
and Disaster.

Very little is known about the life of our greatest
playwright. Into this dearth John Mortimer has
poured out a romping, bawdy, irreverent tale –
whose ingenuity would not have shamed
Shakespeare himself.

John Mortimer QC is the author of five novels,
but is best known as a playwright, writing for the
stage, films and television. His successes include
*The Dock Brief, The Wrong Side of the Park, Two
Stars for Comfort* and *A Voyage Round My
Father* which starred Alec Guinness.

# Will Shakespeare

## John Mortimer

CORONET BOOKS
Hodder and Stoughton

Printed and bound in Great Britain for
Hodder and Stoughton Paperbacks, a
division of Hodder and Stoughton Ltd.,
Mill Road, Dunton Green, Sevenoaks, Kent
(Editorial Office: 47 Bedford Square,
London, WC1 3DP) by
C. Nicholls & Company Ltd.,
The Philips Park Press, Manchester

ISBN 0 340 21979 3

*for*
PENNY, JEREMY AND EMILY MORTIMER

# Contents

Part Three   *"OF COMFORT AND DESPAIR"*

Part Four   *"THE LOVED BOY"*

Part Five   *"REBELLION IN HIS WAY"*

Part Six    *"THE LIVING RECORD"*

# Part One

## "DEAD SHEPHERD"

*"Dead Shepherd now I find thy saw of
  might
'Whoever loved that loved not at first
  sight' "*

As You Like It

# 1

*Being a Prologue Spoken by Me,*
*John "Praise The Lord And Let*
*His Enemies Be Smitten" Rice*

I, JOHN RICE, at one time little Jack Rice, Snotnose, bare arse, runabout Rice, and at one other time, at the best time the Lady Anne, Queen to Crookback Richard, and sweet Viola, fair Rosalind, mad Ophelia and divers other ladies, beautiful, crazed and desirable, until my voice sunk a further octave and I was demoted to Rosencrantz and other attendants, until at the end I became old Adam, old Gloucester and old Hamlet's ghost. Hush, now. Such talk is dangerous. By our new laws you may be flogged for being an actor and declared an Incorrigible Rogue. So let us begin again.

I, John Rice, "Praise the Lord and Let His Enemies be Smitten" Rice, at present sexton, key-holder, grave-tender and singer through the nose on Sundays at the Church of St. Barnaby on the Surrey Bank (no coloured glass, no graven saints, no hassocks nor kneelers and a whipping for any child who sleeps or whispers), I old John Rice being now overstayed three score and ten do wish to set down privately . . . in the utmost privacy . . . (I write with the vestry door double locked, at midnight, with only a glass of thin Communion grape for company) certain recollections of a time that has now gone utterly and will never come again whilst our good masters, who speak daily with the Almighty, obey His direct orders to have the theatres closed and plays forbid. Why did the good God in His Wisdom give such orders? I know not unless He grew jealous, thinking we drew more of the public than even great St. Paul's, and gave better entertainment. (I have writ this last emboldened by Holy Wine. It will never see daylight, I promise you.)

Today, only today, I walked past an old Theatre, near Holywell. The door was chained but I got the old shepherd to unlock for me. I say shepherd because that home of our Battles, our Lovers' Scenes, our Glorious Coronations and Foul Murders, is now the stabling for a flock of woolly sheep, sheared to provide rough shirts for our Puritan masters. The stage, galleries, seats and boxes are torn down by the Ordinance of Parliament. There was a sow littering in the tiring room and on the inner stage I saw a donkey piss against the cobweb shreds of our old arras. But the sheep were orderly. They all stood in the place of the Groundlings, facing the stage with patient vacancy, as though waiting for Dick Burbage to step forward and take them into his confidence. So I stood on the rotting planks of a stage (as I have stood in skirts and painted lips and felt from the ground and the boxes a united throb of lust for my petticoated person) and made a promise to him who gave me My Great Opportunity that I would set down all I knew of him for someone to read, even if it be only me, old Jack Rice, in secret behind the double lock of the vestry door.

So, Shakespeare, this is your book of secrets, writ secretly to be read in private.

You did me a good turn in the year of the Great Plague and I will do this for you, for we became friends when I ceased to be little Jack Sniveller, little Jack Steal-a-penny, and became your principal player of great Queens and sweet boy-girls in breeches. And how I came to that is a story I shall not fear to set down neither, not though it might have me hanged for blasphemy if some of the canting Masters of our Church Council should ever spy these my private papers.

I saw you in my mind's eye today, at the edge of our broken stage or in the ruin of the tiring room, smiling a little, watching carefully and what was in your head? Your fair cut-purse Earl? Your dark boy-girl? Your far-away wife or your silent child? Was your head full of jokes or that fury with which you railed at the Universe? When I have set all down, how much more shall I know you? Well, at least I shall remember.

Will Shakespeare. But to write your name is to hear again the bray of the trumpet and then the sudden silence from the groundlings at the start of a play. And that is a rare reward in these times when a two-hour sermon on the Evils of Fornication is the nearest we come to Comedy.

So I will set it all down before I am dead and you, Will, are quite forgotten.

Now my reader, if times should change by the Grace of God and men suddenly remember that they have an ear for verse and a taste for pleasure, and I have a reader, let me tell you how I shall go to work. Something I saw of Will, when he was at the Theatre, when he was with his pot-girls, and that I can set down of my own knowledge. A lot more I learnt of Dick Burbage and the other actors and of the servants of my Lord Southampton. (It's a wonder what men will do before their servants who, by and large, they regard but as chairs and tables who will not mind their leching, or weeping or quarrelling before them.) Some more I learnt at Stratford when I visited there as an actor and met the neighbours and his most forbearing wife (he called her the "She-Dragon" but when I saw her she had grown old and patient and somewhat lacking in her Dragon's teeth). And some, perforce, I must invent, keeping in my head all I knew of Will and his probable manner at the Court and in the Ale house, of his adventures with Royalty and Harlotry. So as I write out the scenes that follow shall I become, like himself, a playmaker but in secret. What shall I call my play?

"The Tragical, Comical History of King William, with an account of his Conquests, Loves, Struggles, Jealousies, Hatreds and Final Reconciliation with the She-Dragon. As told by John Rice to those who may listen if we get a change of Government."

I can hear my audience scratching, coughing, hawking and spitting. This prologue has gone on too long. Bring on the actors for sweet Christ's sake – or we shall all be off to the Bear-Baiting!

# 2

## Of How Shakespeare Lied About His Life At The Rose Theatre, And How An Honest Man Lost A Capon

WHEN I FIRST knew Shakespeare, he tended the horses outside the old Rose Theatre.

We didn't know he was Shakespeare or where he came from, we didn't even know that he was eaten up with a longing to be inside the Theatre and not at the gate with a load of hay and a spade for gathering dung so it would not foul the red heels of the Lordlings on their way to their seats on the stage. All we knew, he was called "Will" and for a ha'penny he would tend a man's horse while he was at the play.

It was also known that he did this work with commendable efficiency.

At this time I was also working at the Rose. How did the two of us get there, Will, who was twenty-six years old and little Jack Rice, who was then a kind of starveling, underdeveloped twelve, having not yet come to my full tide of beauty and blossomed into a girl? I will tell you shortly.

I was born on a cart travelling the County of Hertford. My mother, God rest her soul (her burial, as you shall hear, was hardly Christian but it was a turning point in my career), sewed the costumes and played the voice of angels for such old Miracle and Morality plays as were done in town squares by the travelling actors on their cart. My father Rice was well known for his portrayal of the Archangel Gabriel, and no doubt because he was of celestial status did not need to enter

into the earthly bonds of matrimony before he got my mother
with child. When I was but a mewler my poor father died of
a sore throat. (They put a noose about his neck when he cut
a purse during a Christmas performance of Noah's Flood in
St. Albans.) Out of respect for his memory my mother took
his name and was always known as "Mistress" Rice, having
indeed been his mistress.

It is no doubt my being whelped by an Archangel which
has helped my survival in these religious times.

My mother had some gypsy blood in her and was the
proud possessor of a handkerchief worked with the design of
a serpent by my Romany grandmother. This token was meant
to bring luck and you shall hear what luck it brought to her
and me and to Master Shakespeare. At the time of my father's
dancing on air out of this world, the actor Ned Alleyn was
playing at St. Albans, and my mother, having little possessions left save the aforesaid handkerchief, Alleyn took her
in with his troop, which was then the Earl of Worcester's
men, as wardrobe mistress; so as a baby I slept sometimes in
a King's fur gown, sometimes in straw. As soon as I was old
enough to stand I was given such great theatrical roles as
scrubbing the stage, shaking the thunder-sheet or emptying
the actors' piss-pots. Nevertheless, I became addicted to the
business: and when Ned Alleyn took over the old Rose
Theatre, well, my mother and I went with him as part of the
company.

And Shakespeare? What had been his history before he
appeared wearing an old red hat and a leather jerkin to tend
the horses outside the theatre? Sure he was not born as I was,
in the shadow of the gallows and the players' cart. His father
was a glove-maker of Stratford, nicely prosperous before debt
began to gnaw away his horde. And Will Shakespeare must
have been comfortable enough in the country, stuffing his
head with all the books he could lay his hand to, and tumbling
whatever wench would go with him "primrose-picking", as
he called it, on the long walk to Shottery. There when he was
but eighteen he tumbled, a big-boned, butter-hair Anne, who
was eight years his senior. "Let still the woman take an elder

than herself," Shakespeare wrote in a play where I did act the breeches part. Perhaps if Anne had been a few years younger she wouldn't have put the fear of God into Shakespeare to make him marry her. Or perhaps it was her family that drove him to the altar; but marry they did in haste one cold November and his wife had a girl, Susanna, in the following May. And then she bore him twins, a girl, Judith, and a son, little Hamnet, who lived to be ... well, you shall hear what he lived to be.

Now family life, they tell me, is not the easiest of conditions. I know not truly because although I have had boy-lovers and girl-lovers, men-lovers and women-lovers pass through my long life for a while, yet I have never had one face to stare at from breakfast time to supper and my only family was my mother who, in spite of her gypsy temper, was a credulous old soul who gave no trouble. Some men solve their family difficulties by being meek and complaisant, some by cuffing the children, kicking the cat and generally terrorising the homestead. Shakespeare's way was the simplest; he moved himself off. Some say the actors came to Stratford, he saw a play and the next day he was gone; but it's my belief he had his plans in head years before that and the getting of his family came only as an enforced interruption.

Now here comes the mystery: and it's only the first one that we shall meet in tracing the Comical, Tragical History of William Shakespeare. After he left Stratford, Will vanished.... Where exactly? Some say he went for a school-master, but I have never heard him speak in the tedious tone of a pedagogue. Some say he worked in an Attorney's office, and there gained his knowledge of bills and leases and fees-tail, and his tight grasp on a handful of money. Dick Burbage once told me Will went for a soldier in the Low Countries, but that was a night of Claret wine and partridges and Dick would remember anything. From time to time I heard Shakespeare swear in the Lingua Italia, and some have said he travelled as far as Verona and Venice where his scenes be set: though I think he got no nearer those hot cities than the sweating pages of Boccaccio.

There was a day when I asked Shakespeare where he spent those years after he left home, and his face went dark and there was a silence which told you that if he gave you an answer it would be a lie, or even a warning to learn your part or mind your acting and not his business. They say the old Knights went into retreat in certain dark monasteries before venturing to battle, and all I can think is that Shakespeare retired into the shadows before assaulting the old Rose Theatre and arriving there as horse-tender. But whether his monastic retreat was a soldier's camp, or lawyer's clerk's office, or even an Italian bordello or stew house by St. Paul's I am not able to tell you. All I know is he came from thence with his head full of the rough ends of a great knowledge of men, women and books and a powerful determination to leap from the dung pile outside the door to the stage inside it.

Now his wife Anne, and two girls, and even his son Hamnet when he began to totter, must have been greatly perplexed to know if they had a father or no. But now and then sums of money would be brought them by travellers or sent in a pedlar's sack from an address unknown. At last Anne got a letter from her husband containing a gold coin he had earned by holding the horses. I have been told of this self-same letter by many parties so I can now repeat it to you, and you may see that whatever skills William had learned in his dark years he had now become a past-master in the art of telling lies.

To my dear wife Anne at Stratford. Wish me well, sweetness. [The letter was somewhat tattered and had a smell of dung which his wife attributed to the Irish pedlar who carried it.] I have been so long silent as my whole strength has been turned on one Object, that of making your Fortune and my Immortality. [With such times off as he turned his strength to making the night beautiful with a pot-girl or a boy lute-player.] Now I have news which will gladden your heart and that of our little family. [When the infant

heard it they say he vomited in disbelief, the others were
more credulous.] Anne, my dear Anne. I am become a voice
in a cry of players. We are set in comfort at the Theatre in
the old Rose Garden at Maiden Lane and every night we
make the rafters ring with the boasts of *Tamburlaine the
Great.* [A fine bloodthirsty piece by one Marlowe whom
you shall hear more of presently. True it did make the
rafters ring but not with any voice of Shakespeare's.] The
groundlings cheer at the terrible tale of the Tyrant and his
captive Queens. [A bad habit of alliteration which he improved later, but it was a phrase to stir the blood in
Stratford.] I must leave writing for I am called for to the
Great Battle scene. [He meant someone had summoned
him to hold a horse's head.] Today I act but for you, and
in memory of your beauty which with God's Grace I shall
behold again when I am given leave of absence by my
audience. Kiss the dear children for me.

Trusting you will share this delight with me and spend
on strong ale and good cheer all of this gold piece :

Yr. loving husband

Will. S.

God knows how these appalling falsehoods did not blister
his hand and burn the paper! And God knows why he should
have chosen such a time, when he was about as close to the
stage as the lad who cleaned a Privy Councillor's boots was
to the Government of England, to suddenly boast of his
alleged success. Perhaps he was lonely and bethought him of
a big-boned, soft-bodied woman with primrose coloured hair
and a smell of milk in a warm bed in Stratford. Perhaps he
thought that by writing down his dreams they might come
true by magic. I can tell you the facts only and what went on
behind the locked doors of that skull, Shakespeare only
knows.

Now the letter was read and re-read by Anne and told to
the children and shown to her brothers, who were openly
scornful and secretly impressed, and to her old Uncle Hathaway, who had once seen a burgomask danced in the court-

yard of Warwick Castle at Christmas and held himself out to be a connoisseur of all matters theatrical. And the neighbours were called in, good Master Hamnet Sadler and his wife Judith. Hamnet Sadler, godfather to the children, after whom young Hamnet Shakespeare was named, was as honest as the skin between his brows and a wool merchant in a small way of business, excellent at the grading of sheep-shearings and knowing the price of flax, but he was a slow scholar and the letter had to be read to him a number of times before he gathered in the news that his old school-fellow and neighbour was now a Great Actor in the city. But when this sunk into his honest skull he was quick with his decision. "When I go into London next month on the wool cart," he promised, "I will call on neighbour William and to celebrate his triumph I will take him a fat Stratford capon reared in my own yard." So then a part of the gold piece was spent on small ale, and Uncle Hathaway brought apricot wine and tried to dance a burgomask, and Judith Sadler grew so warm at the thought of having a neighbour in the Theatre that that night she pulled her hulking husband on top of her and so got their child Francis, him that is now a snivelling Justice of the Peace and devoted to silence on the Sabbath and the flogging of actors.

So it came about that on a warm fine Spring day Hamnet Sadler came to London on the wool cart carrying with him a corn-fed capon to the great actor or minor ostler, depending on whether you look at the matter with Hamnet's eye or the eye of God.

First he went to the Widow Braxton's house at Southwark, an accommodation address where Will had often been accommodated either by that energetic widow woman or her three handsome "daughters", who were related only in their enthusiasm for pressing sheets without a flat iron and their interest in the chinks to be earned by such labour. Shakespeare used this place, among other things, for the writing of letters.

"Master Shakespeare!" Hamnet Sadler stood in the street

and called up at the window of Mother Braxton's evil-
smelling dwelling at the sign of the Grasshopper.

A shutter opened stealthily. A female face of somewhat
tarnished nobility showed itself: behind in the shadows
Hamnet glimpsed younger, creamier countenances and heard
a giggle of laughter.

"I seek Master William Shakespeare. The great actor.
Famous in this town."

"Shake who? I'll shake you, my fine caterwauler." Widow
Braxton was not so bold or so foolish as to ask the names of
her visiting gentry, so all this babble of Shakespeare meant
nothing to her.

"His wife sends me with messages from the country, and
I have a fine capon. Is Master Shakespeare gone to his work
at the Theatre?" Hamnet was puzzled; although it was on
the hop of midday the figures at the window appeared to him
dressed for the night. He was also tired.

"Do but let me step inside and rest my capon. It's a heavy
bird to carry."

At which Hamnet stepped forward to the door and stepped
back quickly and covered his capon as a good half gallon of
slops dropped on him like that gold rainstorm which the
Ancients believed concealed Jupiter the Thunderer. London
folk, Hamnet Sadler had discovered, are nothing near so
friendly as Stratford folk.

So Hamnet Sadler set out to find the Rose Theatre.

Now London was a different sort of place then. If you pass
along the Surrey Bank now, you may find an outdoor prayer
meeting, or one hanging for an offence to Parliament, to entertain you, but then it was all amusement and jollity. Hamnet
had not gone five yards before he was solicited to see the
Bear-Bait, and apes torn to pieces by dogs, or the wonderful
living Mermaid from Gravesend, or the monstrous Blue Giant
of Wapping. He was offered the sight of an old soldier's
wound for a penny, and then told that if he did not pay a
penny he would be shown the self-same wound without
mercy. He was offered half an hour with a certain Lucy
Negro, Abbess de Clerkenwell and a promise he'd never be

hurried for sixpence, and for a shilling he might see a Virgin
from Waltham Cross marry with an ass. At last Hamnet found
a snarling Puritan fellow, father, as I believe, to our own dear
Rector here, who told him, as neighbour Sadler had no reason
to doubt, that the Day of Judgment was at hand. So he asked
the way to the Rose Theatre.

"The theatre is a plague-spot, sir. A wen! A boil which
runs puss and poison infecting us with Idle Dreams of Vanity
and Lust. It is a congregation of rogues and harlots," the
Puritan piped in a high moan of doom and added more
quietly, "Take that lane on the right hand. By London Bridge.
You may nose the actors as you come towards the river."
So Hamnet Sadler went on his way, sniffing like a fox-hound.

\* \* \*

Now the time has come when I must tell a little of the company of actors whom Ned Alleyn had in service, some say
bondage, at the Rose Theatre, at least such as shall play some
part in the events I shall be describing.

First there was Ned Alleyn himself, a tall man who always
wore high red heels and a hat with a long feather to make
himself seem taller. He had a voice like a mighty organ, had
Ned, and someone said an organ as mighty as his voice and,
they added slanderously, fathered so many boys he had to
found a school at Dulwich to get them all educated. He
could roar you one of the poet Marlowe's mighty lines so it
was as grand as a thunderstorm and what matter if you never
understood a word of it. He was a good man though, with
affectations but not affected and I dare say it came as a grief
to him when we all left the Rose to play under the lead of
Dick Burbage.

What can I tell you of Burbage? There is a woman at Old
Street I go to Wednesdays to ease my lusts (gently now, that
weapon has passed its Biblical span and has seen some
service) and I said to her, "Surely you remember Burbage?"
"What was that," she said, "a herb for soups?" Truly he would
have liked a culinary metaphor, for he loved a good dinner

as much as a good play and Shakespeare had to write a line about his fatness when he played Prince Hamlet. Burbage was our leader: he loved the play and he loved players, all but Ned Alleyn, who he said acted like an old she-cow with constipation, which I do not think was fair entirely. Enough of Burbage for now, you shall make his better acquaintance later.

Then there was Sam Crosse, sweet and fat, who kept hens in the grave trap and tethered a goat by the actors' entrance. He loved all animals and played many villains.

Hemminge and Condell were most business-like, they counted the money and paid our wages and helped copy parts, and nagged us like a pair of old aunts if we came to the play in foul hose or stinking of wine or the privy.

Augustine Phillips was a quiet one; he played older women save on a great occasion, which you shall hear more of, when he played Harry the Four and deposed the King of England.

Alex Cooke was a pallid, thin streak of a Puritan, for ever telling us that "All flesh is as the grass" and "Wine is a betrayer" and other matters of which we had rather been kept in ignorance. He would knit the chain-mail for our battle scenes with a big pair of wooden needles. He played the heroines and I longed, child as I was, to have such parts off him. You shall hear how I succeeded.

Also I must tell you of Will Kempe, our clown. A little round tub of a man who could dance and caper light as a thistledown. And then there was William Bell, who could perform as well drunk or sober; though I never saw him put to the test of having to play sober.

One more person I must tell you of, our then poet and chief playmaker, Kit Marlowe. Once, when he was drunk and I was scrubbing the stage, Master Marlowe stuck a rose behind my ear and gave me sixpence because he said I was too ugly for a shilling. The rose-thorn drew blood behind my ear and I was afraid to answer him, having heard he supped each night with the Devil. Truly he was an unbeliever and lucky for him he died before the Puritans conquered England. He had a sort of serving boy, a thin dapper young fellow with a grave-pale face, named Ingram Frizer, who was never from his side. Marlowe and Frizer were showing some of the actors how best to enact a duel scene on the day that good yokel Hamnet Sadler came into the theatre looking for his neighbour Shakespeare and carrying his capon.

"Good day, my Masters," said Hamnet Sadler most respectfully. "I seek Master William Shakespeare!"

"Master William who?" said Marlowe, executing a double passado with his sword and accidentally slicing off the head of the capon.

"Have a care of the capon! Master Shakespeare."

"Shagspar?" said Hemminge, looking down his list of actors. "We have no Shagspar here."

"My Muse is on me . . ." cried Ned Alleyn, shaking off my mother who was trying to fit a new velvet cloak on him. "My Muse is on me and I must rehearse . . ."

"I seek Will Shakespeare." Hamnet gawps up at the towering heels, the sweeping feather and the mighty organ from the groundling position.

"What is that rusty saw," Ned Alleyn squinted vaguely down at him, "that interrupts my music?"

"I seek Master Shakespeare, the great actor. Is he hereabouts?"

"Begone, Shakebean!" Alleyn's arm swept out to dismiss the world, and he went into the mighty *Tamburlaine* which was playing that night.

> "Holla, ye pampered Jades of Asia!
>     What can ye draw but twenty miles a day?
>     And have so proud a chariot at your heels
>     And such a coachman as great Tamburlaine?"

"Not Tammerlain!" Hamnet protested. "The great Shakespeare!"

"Go your ways, turnip-head," said Dick Burbage, not unkindly. "We have no Shakescene here."

"No Shakspar," said Sam Crosse, finding a warm egg in the grave trap.

"No Shagbag, either," said Will Kempe, banging his tabor and cutting a small early-morning caper. "We have no Shagbag at the Rose."

"*Shakespeare!*" Hamnet Sadler felt as any mortal might who strays into a mad house to present a beheaded capon to an actor who didn't yet exist. "I think you have hid my neighbour Shakespeare out of jealousy at his great talents!"

At which Hemminge and Condell threw him out, and his capon with him.

I was rehearsing my usual role of scrubbing the stage at that moment and I laughed heartily, having no more idea than the others who this Shakespeare might be.

\* \* \*

Hamnet Sadler told me, many years after, how he walked through Southwark Market something discouraged. His capon was weighing extremely heavy and he set it down by a horse-trough to sluice his hot face and drink a little. And when he emerged and shook the water from his eyes, lo and behold the capon was gone! And all he saw was a figure in a red hat running swiftly away through the crowds.

By Christ, this London, where a man may not even set down a capon for half a minute whilst he takes a drink!

"Stop thief! Call the Constable! Stop thief!" cried Hamnet, pursuing the red hat like hounds after a scent. The Constable was pleasuring himself up an alley with a whore he had lately arrested and was taking in for a whipping, and the citizens of Southwark paid scant attention.

So through piled apples and between hanging sides of beef and under cart-wheels the chase continued, till Hamnet grabbed the red-hat in a little stinking court by the fish market.

"Got you! You thieving London knave!" said Hamnet and shook his prey as if he were indeed an old hunting dog with Reynardo between his teeth.

And the red hat fell off revealing none other than the great self-styled actor of the Rose Theatre and Hamnet Sadler's neighbour.

"Will! Will Shakespeare!" Hamnet was astonished. "As large as life!"

"Is this yours? Forgive me, Neighbour Hamnet. It's not often a man finds a dinner, abandoned by a Southwark horse-trough."

So Shakespeare bowed and formally handed back the capon, and Hamnet bowed and formally handed it back to him. And, having discovered that his neighbour Sadler was well provided with money Shakespeare suggested they repair at once to the Dagger Inn in Holborn to have that capon cooked and eaten before worse befell it.

# 3

## *Of How Hamnet Sadler Was Severely Disillusioned*

THE DAGGER INN was then the haunt of actors and it was a place like most other places in the world, save Stratford and the neighbouring villages, that knew not the name of Shakespeare. Kate the pot-girl (sharp up-tilted nose, brown hair, a waist small as your hand and a bum moving so it would thaw a Puritan) knew not Shakespeare either, although she was soon to grow familiar with every inch of him. But he appeared to her with money (Hamnet's) and the capon (Hamnet's) and asked her to perform a trick to deceive that same Hamnet Sadler.

"When serving us, for a prank, a merry stratagem," he said, slipping her some more coin of Hamnet's, "bring two cups of wine, bow low over the table and say 'Master Shakespeare, with the compliments of your fellow actors.'"

"Shake what?" said Kate the pot-girl, anxious to oblige.

"'Speare'. And I pray you. Try to remember the name."

So Shakespeare went back to Hamnet while they waited for the capon's breast to turn brown upon the spit, and in poured the actors: Ned Alleyn with his plumes nodding like a funeral horse something past its prime, and Dick Burbage, Sam Crosse and the rest, and me, little Jack Rice, brought to run errands if needed and allowed to finish the musty quarter inches at the end of an occasional bottle.

Hamnet recognised the actors, and was pained and surprised they never cracked a smile or passed the time of day with their great colleague, William Shakespeare.

"There be your actors! Why, they never glanced at you, Will."

"There is much jealousy in the theatre. My applause a little outdid theirs, after my death scene . . ." Shakespeare sounded as if he cared not a fig for the actors.

"Your death scene, Will?"

"O, surely, I die often, as the tyrant Tamburlaine."

"Dang it! I must go home on the wool cart tomorrow. Would you had died today!"

"Today we had a jig and a bawdy tale, done by the minor players." The time had clearly come to nip Hamnet's interest in the theatre in the bud. "But tell me now, Neighbour Hamnet, the news from Stratford. . . . How fares that Imperious Majesty my good wife Anne? How does the She-Dragon?"

"Why, well, Will. Saving every penny you send her."

"Would she spent them! They're hard enough to find."

"Not for you, Will! I have read your letter. . . . Not for the Great Player of London."

Enough of that; Shakespeare moved back to safer ground. "And the children?"

"You daughter Susanna can sing you a catch, and bake a pastry. As for young Hamnet . . ."

"My young rascal? How does he?" The boy had been but a year old when his father removed himself from his parental responsibilities, but Shakespeare either felt, or did he think he ought to feel, the rub of the chain of loving which they say binds a man to his son, as the only hope that his name may be carried into the misty future.

"I wish he were a rascal, Will. The boy is of the silent sort. I reckon he misses his father."

But before young Hamnet could be discussed further, Kate the pot-girl came up and set two cups of wine on the table saying (a perfect performance both in the triumph of being word-perfect in the name, and in the bow which gave both men such a sight of her bubbies as determined Will Shakespeare to devise her better acquaintance and set

Hamnet Sadler thinking of his amorous concerns in the county of Warwickshire), "Master Shakespeare, with the compliments, sir, of your fellow actors."

"Dang me but I misjudged them," Hamnet said. "After all, they do know their master!"

\* \* \*

At our actors' table Ned Alleyn was, as usual, talking. "In his new piece ... I tell you, lads, Marlowe has writ me a death speech of some fifty verses ... Think of it ... fifty verses 'ere death overtakes me as Doctor Faustus!"

Burbage, who in those hungry days said what he thought rather than what would keep the company happy, muttered, "Pray God death doesn't overtake us too before you're finished!"

"Dick Burbage!" Alleyn was outraged. "Because you gabble your lines together do not think there is not a proper way of making music, with the vocal organ!"

"I try to imitate the speech of human beings."

"That's not the way, dolt. We are not 'human beings'. We are not pygmies!"

We all knew what Alleyn expected of us and sang out in unison, "We are *heroes!*"

"Must we over-play to be heroic?" Burbage was brave, in those days, as I have told you.

Alleyn, his huge plumes nodding, swept his arm to appeal to the great wide world to witness his genuine bewilderment. "Over-play? *Over-play?* What is over-play?" And as his gaze roved the room he, and indeed all of us, were astonished to see a red-faced yokel rise from a neighbouring table with a glass in his hand and an apparent expression of extreme gratitude.

"Dang it, that be kindly of you, actors!" Hamnet Sadler was genuinely moved. "That be generous!"

He sat down, it seemed pulled back to his place by his friend and neighbour, and Ned Alleyn vaguely and graciously returned his salutation. So we sat drinking and talking of how

Master Kit Marlowe might be induced to actually finish his *Tragical History of Doctor Faustus*. The whole play would only be writ, Ned Alleyn knew from bitter experience, if the poet Marlowe were kept from girls, strong drink and his constant curling-boy, hair-dryer and sneerer in corners, young Master Ingram Frizer.

"I will lock him in my room," Ned Alleyn told us. "A day and a night together! There's no other way with authors."

The man who was to become such an author, and so suitable for incarceration, was now having to deal with a request from his neighbour Sadler whose blood had been something heated by the strong sack and the sight of the stooping pot-girl.

"You are a past-master at writing letters, Will." Hamnet was looking enviously at his neighbour. "Would I were a past-master at writing letters!" He leant forward confidentially. "There's a certain young widow-woman that works in the dairy at Wasperton. A man cannot do but love her, Neighbour Will."

"What, even a married man, Neighbour Hamnet?"

"Even a married man must have his feelings."

At which moment Kate swung past so close he could feel the warmth of her belly through her petticoats, so Shakespeare felt bound to agree.

"If I could but tell that widow-woman how I loved her then she must yield to me, but I lack words, Will. I have it all but the words . . ."

"Kate. Pretty Kate, bring us a quill, ink and paper." Shakespeare was about to exercise his talents for composition.

"Want to write a play, do you, Master Shakepiece?" Kate, her part played, was now bubbling with laughter.

When the quill arrived Shakespeare touched the point to remove any clinging dust or hair, sucked the feather's end as I have seen him do a thousand times, and started to give the matter thought.

"Works in the dairy, does she?" He began to write, "O, widow of Wasperton, you with breasts of churned butter and thighs of creamed milk . . ."

Not his best work, undoubtedly, but Neighbour Hamnet was delighted with the composition. "A fine phrase!" he said. "Such a phrase and she must surrender! It will break her defences so I may invade her."

*            *            *

Hamnet Sadler was still delighted with his letter, and having looked it over some ninety times was almost able to decipher its mysteries, as he rode home on the wool cart next day to Stratford. He had spent a night in what was less a room than a sort of hay loft. This same loft, Shakespeare told him, was where he slept on such nights as he was too drunk to face his landlady in that rich lodging he, of course, kept as befitting a leading actor.

Now as ill luck would have it the wool cart, on its trundle out of the city, passed the old Rose Theatre and Hamnet raised his eyes from his precious paper long enough to see his neighbour William at work, not tearing to shreds the passions of the Mighty Tamburlaine, not driving Captive Kings between the shafts of his chariot, not riding in Triumph through Persepolis, but making a neat pile of horse dung and straw during the afternoon performance. So Hamnet stopped the cart and ran across to the Humble Ostler who touched his old red hat without bothering to look up from the steaming droppings.

"Mind your horse, Master?"

Hamnet was looking at his neighbour, as angrily disillusioned as a fond father who returns home to find the daughter he believed a tremulous virgin pressing the orchard grass with the gardener's boy.

"You are a *horse tender*, Will!"

"For the moment." Shakespeare had no choice but to admit it. "Just for the moment. They will give me work inside presently."

"Lies!" Hamnet thundered. "Damn lies! You told us you were an actor!"

"I work at the Theatre. They were no lies – a pardonable exaggeration."

"You lied to your good wife!"

"Lying to wives is often the kindest thing you can do for them. Now, good Neighbour Hamnet . . ."

"Damn me! Your wonderful letter! Lies!" Hamnet was still appalled by the enormity of the deception.

"The truth of our dreams is no less true than . . ." Shakespeare was about to explain something of great import in his thoughts on the drama poetic, but Neighbour Hamnet interrupted brutally.

"I'll have to tell Anne; I can't keep the truth from her!"

It was then Shakespeare saw the precious letter to the widow of Wasperton peeping from Hamnet's doublet. Smiling, he quoted scripture. "Great is the truth and mighty above all things." And so he plucked the letter from its hiding place. "For, if we're having the truth, now, shall I tell your wife Judith the truth about you and the Widow of Wasperton – her with the . . ." Shakespeare's actor's hands described two crescents in the air, ". . . of churned butter and the . . ." Hamnet saw his neighbour's hands again lovingly caress the morning around them, and on the other side of the street the already moving wool cart was impatient to continue its journey back to Stratford. "Of creamed milk? Now, Hamnet!" Shakespeare was triumphant. "Shall I write another letter home with news of your doings in the dairy?"

There wasn't much of what we actors call a pause before Hamnet had made his country mind up. "Happen we best both keep silent," he said.

"Happen we best!" Shakespeare restored the widow's letter to its nest in Hamnet's doublet.

"But it was unneighbourly of you, to tell me lies, Will."

"It was unneighbourly of you to find me out."

"God forgive you, Will."

And Hamnet ran to jump on the tail of the wool cart with Shakespeare calling after him, defiant, "Today's lies will be truth tomorrow!"

# 4

## Of How Ned Alleyn
## Engaged A Cock-Crow

You will want to know how Will Shakespeare entered the theatre. Then, I will tell you. He entered it by climbing the roof about dawn one fine Summer morning a month or two after the events which I have herein before related.

You may picture our Rose Theatre: and you had best picture it, for it no longer has existence even as a sheep pen or sty for porkers. Our first playhouse was in shape octagonal, of construction wood and plaster on a brick foundation, of roofing thatched. Roses, red, white, pink and butter-coloured still grew in plenty round the gate. Within was the jut of apron stage open to the rain and hail-stones if we offended God, or to the eggs and rotten cabbages if we did not please the common fellows who stood on the ground before us. Better class of citizens sat round in the galleries and Knights, Lords or those with money to fee the gate-keeper sat sometimes on the stage itself. Behind an arras was an inner stage and over this inner stage a tower-like structure divided as to the first storey balconies on which actors could appear "above"; second storey the private room for the conning of parts both of plays and potgirls by our Master Ned Alleyn; third storey for a window out of which one blew a trumpet at the start of the performance; and rooftop on which a flag emblazoned with the device of a Rose in bloom flew when there was a play forward.

Below the stage there was the big tiring room where all

the clothes were stitched by my patient mother and a carpenter's shop for the cobbling up of thrones, beds, coffins and other properties. Off this room a kind of cupboard in which slept Master Jack Rice the scrub-boy, keeping company with a tribe of elderly and somewhat docile rats.

Within this eight-sided castle the actors did sleep, quarrel, play and, when luck offered, fornicate. Without it Will Shakespeare minded the horses and longed to break its barricadoes.

It was, it seemed, a low point in his career when, having sent a purse of horse-minding money to Stratford, Shakespeare was out of a lodging and sleeping in a cart of straw by the horse rail. He woke early, there's nothing like sleeping in a heap of straw to promote early rising, the ticks, fleas and creeping mice calling you at dawn; and he looked up at the thatched castle wall of the Rose Theatre, now locked secure against all invaders.

But to stand upon that stage was the top of his ambitions.

So he climbed, out of the straw, up the old ash tree, clung to the thatch and slithered down to the third gallery, dropped to the second and so, with a leap, was in the centre of that jutting platform which was to be the world where he was both confined and liberated.

Now he had trapped among the rubbish that fouled the entrance a discarded page, copy of that great last canonade of a speech which was most of all that our poet Marlowe had yet writ of the *Tragical History of Doctor Faustus*. So, having committed it to memory Shakespeare intoned some of these verses in a fair imitation of Ned's mighty organ (vocal).

> "Adders and serpents let me breathe awhile
>     Ugly hell, gape not: come not Lucifer!
> (Being alone, here he snatched at his own throat as if to drag
> himself down to the everlasting roasting)
>     O Mephistophelis!"

So he died and got no applause for it, for to tell truth, we were all fast asleep.

But he was triumphant, at his first speech given on any stage, so in that triumph, being first, and perhaps last, a country boy, a yokel, a bumpkin, he opened his mouth and with a cunning born of many a morning waking in a farm-yard or under a hedgerow after some night of loving, Will Shakespeare crowed him like a cock.

Now there be cock-crows and cock-crows. Those made by the bird in person no doubt have the genuine country tone to them (I do not hold myself out as a great expert in the matter, being all my conscious life a yokel of that fine farming land which lies between Tower Wharf and St. Paul's) but when your ordinary mortal does a cock-crow he produces, as I understand, but a feeble and forced "Doodle Doo" which has little of the roost of morning or the treading, feather-fluff-ing trumpet of triumph and scream of virility produced by your natural model. Now William's cock-crow was so real, so life-like and yet a little more coloured, a thought more glorious, in fact, more of the theatre theatrical, than could have been managed by any mortal bird.

Alleyn's head stuck out of his window. Where the rest of him was or with whom I know not. Strangely enough he was smiling with every appearance of delight.

"Who is there?" he thundered. "Who is this warbler?"

The actors sleeping in the galleries began to stir and poke their heads over.

Once again, by way of an encore and for no better reason than he had stood upon a stage reciting verses, Shakespeare gave them another taste of Chanticleer.

And so the actors came stumbling out to him, yawning, scratching, rubbing sleep from their eyes. And as my gypsy mother unfolded herself from the cocoon of Royal Robes in which she kept swaddled and Sam Crosse prepared to milk the goat, as William Kempe pissed secretly up against the side of the stage and Alex Cooke reared out of his bed like a white worm prodding its small head from the earth to see if any blackbirds be passing and as I, little Jack Rice, crawled from my cupboard blinking into the daylight, we all heard Ned Alleyn give the Ostler a most unexpected welcome.

"Well, horse-tender, would you join us, lad, in the *Tragical History of Doctor Faustus?*"

Shakespeare could scarce believe his ears and replied modestly, "I know a line or two of your new Tragedy."

Alleyn was hard of hearing and, as I believe, his nether limbs were engaged by some visitor. He boomed, "Speak up!"

"I know a line or two of that same Faustus' speech."

"Do you, by God!" said Alleyn. "A learned horse-tender!"

"'O Soul be changed into water drops ...'" Shakespeare intoned in his best Ned Alleyn manner,

"'... and fall into the ocean, ne'er be found!'"

"A poetic horse-tender!" Alleyn swore and we all laughed dutifully. Burbage threw a prompt for the next line,

"'Adders and serpents ...'"

"'Adders and serpents, let me breathe awhile!'" Shakespeare was staring, wide-eyed, into his imaginary Underworld.

"'Ugly hell, gape not: come not, Lucifer!
I'll burn my books: O Mephistophelis

At which he was acting with such a paroxysm of eyes rolling, staggering, coughing and spluttering that Burbage was hard put to it to conceal his mirth and warned, "Be careful, Ned. This lad's going to steal your thunder!"

"Excellent, boy!" Ned Alleyn was exceedingly generous. "Your line will come after that."

"My line ... ?"

"The cock-crow that marks the dawn. Pipe up, then!"

It was comical how the Ostler's face fell when he began to guess how he was parted. "I am to play ... a cock-crow?"

Whereat my mother, measuring-tape round her neck, bustled up to take his measurements. "Will he need a costume?" she asked Alleyn.

"No costume, Mistress Rice. He'll be behind the curtain. What, would you dress him in feathers?"

And William Kempe, replacing some of his liquid with a filled can of small ale, moved up to offer Shakespeare a gulp.

"Drink, horse-tender; you are promoted to a noise behind the curtain!"

It was some promotion from his Ostlerhood certainly, and Shakespeare drank to it, with a smile as sweet as a crab apple.

"Now, once again, for all to hear. Give us your roust of morning." Alleyn couldn't have enough of this performance and, his throat filled with small ale and his heart a little lifted now he was at last inside the Rose's guarded octagon, Shakespeare crowed them to shatter the heavens. Burbage started the applause and we all joined in as if we had just seen Will Kempe dance a Burgomask or Ned Alleyn die.

"Is it not rare?" Alleyn was delighted once more.

"Oh, rare cock-crow!" Will Bell drank a health to our new noise-off.

"It will delight Kit Marlowe, that I promise you!" Alleyn beamed and retired to the delights of his bed chamber.

"And I would," Shakespeare muttered, not without rancour, "that Master Marlowe were here to listen to a sound so natural and unforced."

# 5

## Of the Poet Marlowe, And How He Imprisoned Shakespeare

I HAVE TOLD you of our then playmaker Marlowe, and how he scratched my neck with the thorn of a rose, and indeed he struck as much fear into my child's heart as if he had been the Devil himself. My mother, God rest her if ever He comes to hear of her demise, was indeed convinced that Marlowe was the Devil, and if he passed her would take infinite precautions of crossing herself, lifting three closed fingers before her face, spitting down wind, holding up twigs of Rosemary and drinking a brew of rosehips and myrtle berries to ward off the Evil Eye. But as I have said his evil eye was all for his body servant (never was description more apt) Ingram Frizer; and he surely never noticed my mother or me sufficiently to cast his curse upon us.

Kit Marlowe the shoemaker's son had got a head start by coming to Cambridge University and a fair gentleman's education. It was said that at Cambridge (a place I never went to and it may be where Beelzebub is accustomed to buy the souls of all students for aught I know of it) he both learned to doubt God and to sell his services as a spy to the pay of gentlemen close to the Privy Council. It is certain he became a friend of young Thomas Walsingham, whose uncle, Sir Francis, was high in the plots of Her old Majesty and an arch conniver and double-dealer in the service of the Crown. Will Shakespeare told me that Marlowe was a playmaker who used words like cannonades but could never make a joke or create a human being; the first his life was too filled to leave time for and the second he left to that God whose handiwork he, on mature consideration, despised. Yet William told me he could not have gone on his journey had not Marlowe cut a way for him; and he called Kit his shepherd, although if ever there were such a shepherd in wolf's clothing I have yet to hear of it.

I will rise to make sure the vestry door is double fastened and the shutter closed before the window before I dare write some of the sayings of this same Marlowe. There now. We are safe. Let me dare the Rector, and the sidesmen and the Council and all the Parishioners, not to speak of the Parliament representing the Almighty, and write down some of the sayings of this devilish poet.

But first let me remember him, finely dressed in sombre velvets with gold lace and a glittering ear-ring and buttons far beyond his station. His lower lip was full and soft, his eye brown and beckoning, his smile dangerous, his hair dark or reddish, depending on the industry of Frizer and the supply of henna. He would sit among the actors in the Dagger with Frizer beside him and I squatted on the ground, for when Marlowe gave Frizer an errand, why then Frizer would give me a stir with his little pointed boot and send me to run it for him. Truly I was too alarmed to heed the poet's words, but in after years the actors have reminded me of them.

"Truly, the Lord God," Marlowe used to say, "only invented the Holy Ghost so they might have a third to play Primero."

Or, "For my part I find Communion wine too sweet, and once I asked at the altar rails for a pipe of tobacco instead."

Or, "Christ loved no woman, saving all his sport for John the Baptist."

Or, "If I had to invent a religion, I would do a finer work than either God or Jesus, whose conceits but led to men's slaughter of each other and much burning at the stake."

Or, "St. Paul was a notable Juggler and the Archangel Gabriel a bawd, who arranged an afternoon bedchamber mating betwixt the Virgin Mary and the Holy Ghost."

Whether these remarks discomforted God I know not, but they certainly terrified the actors.

Not that Marlowe came often among us. As I have told you he was much beloved of young Thomas Walsingham and he and Frizer sat less often at the stained deal of the Dagger Inn than at Sir Francis Walsingham's polished mahogany where he would drink fire waters and light his long clay pipe and vow that the wooden "O" of the Theatre was too small a cockpit for his talents, and that he longed to tangle in the plots of living persons, to be privy to the great Drama of the State; there he would sell his soul for the good of the Kingdom and not a mere penny entrance from the groundlings.

You will remember, any of you who have grown to years of discretion such as three score and ten (and if they really were discreet years would I be committing one syllable of all this blasphemy to paper?), that our Great Opponent in those distant days was the King of Spain, and he was at all times eager to poison our Monarch, topple the throne and capture our Estate through the Machievel plottings of his Catholic adherents here in England. Now I believe that not all English Catholics were in the pay of his Twisted Majesty. I believe some of them preferred their Mass to other Ecclesiastical Diversions, as some men take poultry instead of beefs, or love tall slender girls better than the short and comfortable; but however that may be, the eager old Sir Francis Walsingham had only to hear the distant echo of an Ave Maria or the clatter of beads and he bethought of plots and poisonings and foul treachery that must be rooted out by him on behalf of Her Majesty's Council. And to sniff such treachery he needed a spy whose wit and soft under lip would make him a welcome guest in secret Catholic houses. So he chose none other than that cunning contriver of tales dramatic, the poet Christopher Marlowe.

Of course such a plot was not so complex or well woven as to hold the straying attention of the poet for long. Marlowe needs must out-Machievel Machievelli and take his fee for spying on the Council from the Catholics as well as spying on the Catholics for the Council. And this I heard on the authority of none other than the man who was once under-butler to old Sir Francis Walsingham, who was present when that same curling-boy, confidant and catamite, Ingram Frizer, was summoned privily and fee'd by the Walsinghams to spy on his master Marlowe and report on his double-dealing. So have you ever heard of such a circle of spies all spying on each other? Marlowe and Frizer had purses well laden and dressed in finer velvets and lace as a result of all this private activity but, as you shall discover, it ended not well: and it's my opinion that a playmaker had best confine his plottings to the Theatre. This was a lesson Shakespeare also had to learn hardly in years to come.

So what of Shakespeare whilst Marlowe laughed and balanced his life on the point of a dagger and changed once again the colour of his hair and was daily drunk not on Rhenish wine (although he and Frizer drank deep of that from breakfast to bedtime) but on the joy of all his dangers, and the success met by his *Tragical History of Doctor Faustus* which drew in Lords and groundlings, crowns and pennies, thanks to the roll of its poetry, the music of Ned Alleyn and a startling cock-crow which heralded the dawn after the Doctor's Death and Damnation. Well, Shakespeare was given some other tasks about the theatre, all behind the arras and outside the view of the public. He had the list of cues pinned on his doublet as he stood at the point of entry, he took some part in the lighting of the fireworks and I gave him instruction in the proper management of the thunder-sheet. Ned Alleyn paid him, or promised to pay him (with Alleyn the mere mention of money was enough to discharge a debt) what he earned as an Ostler with a little addition. But I cannot say his ambitions were fully satisfied as Chanticleer and he has said that he stood each night in torment, listening to the play of Faustus and knowing how it might be done better.

Now Shakespeare had not encountered Marlowe until one afternoon when our newest actor was standing awaiting his cue. Marlowe had been sent for by Ned Alleyn, who wished to discuss with his playmaker the question of Doctor Faustus' successor. So, as Shakespeare stood behind the curtain, came a figure in fine velvets swaggering up to him who, after sending Ingram off for a supply of wine of better quality than we had in the cellars of the Rose, accosted him as Doctor Faustus performed his final agonies on the stage.

"How now, boy!" Marlowe could see no other person ready to engage in trouble, so his company was forced on Shakespeare.

"Hush talking, boy. I'll miss my cue." Shakespeare started to strike midnight on an old rusty bell.

> "It strikes! It strikes! Now body turn to air
> Or Lucifer will bear thee straight to hell!"

They heard Alleyn booming from the stage.

"What are you? A one-liner?"

Instead of answering Marlowe, Shakespeare dived for the thunder-sheet and shook it just in time.

> "O soul be changed into small water drops,"

Alleyn had been waiting for the thunder.

> "And fall into the ocean ne'er be found."

"You have a line, have you? One of the two and a half thousand lines of this beautiful play."

Shakespeare turned to look at this Exquisite who seemed no older than he, but who was dressed like a Duke and smelt of sweet musk and pomander. He was in an ill-humour with Dr. Faustus that day.

"This play! Two and a half thousand lines and not one jest!"

At which Marlowe, his hand on his dagger, moved so his face was within an inch of Shakespeare's.

"No jests! Did you say ... no jests?"

"My God! My God! Look not so fierce upon me!" came the cry of Alleyn from the stage.

"'Enter devils with fireworks. They run about,'" Shake-

speare quoted with some contempt. "That is all the author
wrote. They laugh at forked tails and gunpowder, scarcely at
the author's wit."

"You know who the author is . . . ?" The dagger was moving
up its sheath in Marlowe's hand.

"Why, one Christopher Marlowe. His lines are all stage-
thunder and the lightening of tallow candles."

"I'll burn my book . . . O Mephistophelis!" Ned Alleyn
held his breath on stage, waiting for a cock-crow that didn't
come.

"You shall suffer for that, boy!" Marlowe had Shakespeare
by the collar and his dagger out. This Marlowe thought most
literary matters might be solved by an inch or two of steel
applied under the ribs.

"O Mephistophelis!" Ned Alleyn repeated, not altogether
patiently, from the stage.

Whereupon Shakespeare opened his mouth and let out a
sound like all the devils released from Hell, the rudest, loudest, craziest cock-crow of his life. Whereat Marlowe dropped
his dagger and Alleyn, in full fig as Dr. Faustus, came off the
stage followed by a thunder of applause.

"So, you are come! I sent for you yesterday. Leave murder-
ing our Chanticleer, Christopher. It's the best cock-crow in
the theatre."

"Christopher? You are Master Marlowe?" Shakespeare
seemed not over discomforted.

'Yes, boy. So, my play's have no jests to them?"

"No jests. But some fine lines, and . . ." Shakespeare sought
one deliberately, " 'Make ready my coach, my chair, my
jewels . . .' That's a fine death line for the mad Queen in
*Tamburlaine*."

"So, something meets your approval . . ." Marlowe said
sourly.

"It had some truth."

The dagger moved up the sheath another inch.

"Kit, are you drunk or sober?" Alleyn hated bloodshed
except in a play.

"Drunk! Else I had pricked this blown-up bladder of conceit," said Marlowe.

Alleyn sighed. "How often have I to tell you, Kit? One doesn't duel with actors! Actors are not gentlemen, unless they play Kings, of course. Certainly not if they play cocks, behind the curtain!"

At which Marlowe was forced to laugh and the dagger slid back to sleep. Alleyn, one arm round his poet's shoulder, strolled him away.

"Now, we have so much gunpowder left over. What do you say to a Chronical Historical? Our subject: The Wars of York and Lancaster, I to play that sainted Monarch, Harry the Sixth!"

Shakespeare was listening, trying to remember that ineffectual King.

\* \* \*

I remember one afternoon when the Theatre was riven by a cry of triumph. I was helping my mother fold and press the tirings when Shakespeare came to us shouting that Alex Cooke had a gum boil and, the great part of the third student falling vacant, he, William, was parted in it. Never have I seen such rejoicing over a gum boil! So Shakespeare went off to try a hundred ways of saying his lines and, going up to the balcony for quiet, he heard a thunder of knocking. He had learnt enough of our theatre to know what it was. Master Marlowe had been somewhat laggard in dispatching the Sixth Harry, and our leading actor had had him locked into his room until at least one Part was done.

"Help! Let me out!" Shakespeare smiled and climbed the steep steps to Alleyn's door. He noticed a key hanging outside it: but he had no intention of releasing the Prisoned Poet. He came there with the unworthy intention of having his revenge on a man who had near frightened him to death with his dagger.

So, Shakespeare told me, was this scene played on either

side of a locked door, as the imprisoned Marlowe called again
on Shakespeare for his release.

"I am forbid, on pain death, to let you out."

Marlowe was puzzled by the voice without. "Who is that?"

To which he received by way of an answer a triumphant
"Cock-a-doodle-do!"

And Marlowe remembered. "Lord Rooster! Half a crown
if you let me out, little cock-crow!"

Shakespeare told him that he was not to be corrupted and
as a new actor he had the good of the Theatre at heart. The
play must be completed.

"Devil take the play!" Marlowe shouted. "I am engaged to
meet a great Lord, one that might do you a service."

"Poor girl, she will be disappointed." Shakespeare was
enjoying the scene mightily.

"And you blame me for ill jests. Let me out, I tell you!"
Another huge rattle on the handle.

"When you have writ your stint, Master Marlowe. Write
away, good Master Marlowe."

"Write? How can I write this dull quarrel between Brain-
less Barons?"

"True, I have noticed your verse sometimes walks a little
halting," said Shakespeare then safely critical.

This provoked a fine bellow of, "Open the door that I may
rip your belly!"

Almost a-hop with pleasure Shakespeare answered, "What
sort of a bribe is that?"

Now Marlowe tried the appeal pathetic. "To write a scene
locked in on a diet of dry ink and paper. Impossible! How
would you like it?"

"I might try to work it." Shakespeare was seriously considering the matter.

"Would you? My Lord Impertinent!" But when he had his
final shout the devious and cunning mind of Marlowe, the
great plot-maker, got to work and he bethought him of a
stratagem which might gain him his release at last. He went
to the door and spoke softly, with much courtesy. "But, of

course, you have a taste for a plot. The nice judgment of a line...."

"Have I so?" Shakespeare was puzzled but didn't argue the matter.

"When we first met you showed yourself Lord Critical."

"Did I so? Perhaps, if you told me where you are defeated ...?"

"The scene is in Temple Gardens."

"What plays there?" Shakespeare was eager, he was nearer than a cock-crow to the making of a play.

"The Barons are quarrelling. Before they pluck roses, they ask Lord Warwick to decide between them."

"Lord Warwick." Shakespeare was thoughtful. "He'd speak in the voice of my own county."

"So, by good fortune, you can help me. Here is the line before. Somerset speaks. 'Judge you ... my Lord of Warwick then between us ...?' Now tell me, Rooster. What should Warwick's answer be? Remember, they're two identical factions of Baronial Bully boys with nothing to choose between them ..."

Shakespeare was thinking, ensnared by the problem. He made his suggestion. "Like two equal hawks, or dogs, even."

"A good image! Now, give me the line." Encouragement came from behind the locked door.

"In verse?"

"If you can, crow me a stanza."

Had he always thought in verses? I know not, but Shakespeare spoke them quickly now. "'Between two hawks — which flies the highest pitch?'"

"What?" Marlowe, ever cunning, affected not to hear.

Shakespeare spoke louder. "Between two hawks!"

Grinning behind the door Marlowe repeated, "I cannot perfectly hear you."

"'Between two hawks, which flies the highest pitch ...?'" Shakespeare bawled.

"I cannot hear!" Marlowe bawled back.

So, furiously, intent on creation, Shakespeare grabbed the key, opened the door, and walked straight into the spider's trap. Half an hour later he was sat at the table roughing a speech with quill and paper, whilst Marlowe stood respectful by. Shakespeare sucked the end of his feather, leant back and read what he had written, still in the boom of Alleyn.

> "Between two hawks, which flies the higher pitch?
> Between two dogs, which has the deeper mouth?
> Between two girls, which has the merriest eye?"

He looked nervously at Marlowe for approval. "How does it run?"

"Run? It capers! Lord Ingenious!" Marlowe was full of praise, which Shakespeare was delighted to accept.

"Thank you, my Lord Stuck!"

"You have leaped from the barnyard to Parnassus in one jump! An ambitious rooster. What do you long for, most?"

"To be ..."

"The truth now!"

"One of my Lord Strange's players and to lend my hand with the playmaking."

The key was on the table and Marlowe's hand fell on it covertly. His voice was reassuring. "Then take my place. Work at it now. No wine, no lewd girls or boys like fawns. Just dry ink and unsensual paper." He went out as Shakespeare fell to writing, mouthing the words as he wrote them.

> "Between two girls, which has the merriest eye?
> But in these nice, sharp quillets of the law,
> Good faith, I am no wiser than a daw."

"Is that a lame rhyme, Kit?"

He asked the question, but there was no answer. He looked round and the room was empty. He had no choice but to finish the Act, for when he tried the door he found Marlowe had locked it on his way out, and he was a prisoner. Since that day, he told me, he felt a prisoner always, condemned to the lonely task of driving a black quill across an empty paper.

# 6

## Of How Two Playmakers Accosted
## A Constable And Shakespeare
## Brought His Work For Approval

HARRY THE SIXTH'S First Part was received with more cheers
than *Faustus* and as many as *Tamburlaine* and drew in more
solid chinking coins than either, nor was it a secret that Marlowe's talent was spent in bright chatter and dark dealings in
the houses of the Walsinghams, and it was Will Shakespeare
who was kept locked at Alleyn's table with nothing but a
faint-hearted saintly King and a horde of bloodthirsty barons
for company. Shakespeare brought news of their success to
Marlowe in the Dagger where Christopher was in a corner
with one arm round Kate the pot-girl and the other about the
thin shoulders of Ingram Frizer. Flushed with victory
Shakespeare said, "They listened, Kit, so still you might
hear . . ."

"A groundling fart?"

"And at the end they cheered!" Shakespeare ignored the
rudeness.

"And threw up their sweaty nightcaps!"

Marlowe looked at a corner of the tavern where Kate's
husband Tom, a huge rogue who worked the wherry boats,
was asleep before the fire. Then Marlowe pushed Kate into
Shakespeare's arms and bade her content "the little playmaker" and help him celebrate his hour of triumph. So while
Marlowe returned to his natural delight in Ingram Frizer,
Shakespeare had Kate in his arms and had let his hands
weigh the size of her bubbies and his tongue venture into the

little dark and perfumed cave of her mouth, before the huge water boatman awoke with a roar and advanced on the new playmaker with a meat cleaver, intent on confining that dramatist's performed works to one, and his future to the next five minutes.

Seeing this, Marlowe, working *ex tempore*, devised a quick exit through the window, and Ingram Frizer, first upsetting a bench to halt Husband Tom's progress, leaped after them.

So it came that two playmakers, ornaments of the Rose Theatre, with all their fine stanzas awash in their brains, were running fugitive in the night when there rose up before them the fat and dignified figure of a Constable, holding up his rod of office.

"How now, Bully Boys! Drunken Revellers! What, will you spoil the sleep of good people with your Hillooing through the night?" This man was Nicholas, Constable of the Watch, and he spoke with such enormous, rumbling dignity that you would think he doubled the office with that of Pope of Rome, Holy Roman Emperor, Archbishop of Canterbury and Rouge Dragon, Herald Extraordinary. "I will apprehend you now," Constable Nicholas proceeded solemnly to sentence, "for a pair of outrageous benefactors. Your names, if you please, the pair of you."

Marlowe swept off his hat, bowing politely. "I am St. John the Baptist. This is my friend St. Joseph of Arimathaea."

The look of purple outrage on the constable's face grew darker. His voice sank another octave. "St. John, sir," he rumbled, "I suggest you are being candid!"

"No, sir," said St. Shakespeare of Arimathaea, also bowing with the utmost politeness. "We are lying in our teeth."

"Don't trifle with me, sir. I am Nicholas, Constable of the Watch!"

"Then are you," Shakespeare bowed again, "a most idiotic and ridiculous piece of pomposity!"

"Pomposity?" Constable Nicholas was delighted. "Ay, I am that. Thanks be to God."

"And a cringing, creeping, time-serving Popinjay!" Marlowe bowed lower than Shakespeare; and Constable Nicholas was almost overcome by such flattery.

"I do serve time pretty well, sir. I thank you for it."

"And an arrogant and a pontifical Simpleton," Shakespeare added, smiling.

"Simpleton? I try to be, sir."

"Oh, worthy and respectable Constable." Marlowe bowed and came up smiling. But this time he had contrived to insult the Constable. The purple hue returned, his voice rumbled in the bit of his belly.

"*Respectable?* You call me *respectable!* What, you man of integrity! Would you insult the Queen's officer? Call out the Watch now! Call out the Watch!"

The Constable pulled out his whistle to call out the Watch and the two Saints took to their heels. And while they pounded down one alley, round two corners and up another they wondered a moment that there was no pursuit. In fact, Ingram Frizer had stepped out of a doorway on hearing Nicholas' whistle, and used his ever eager dagger to silence that Officer. This I had from one that scrubbed floors at the Dagger, but I know not the truth of it as the Coroner never learnt the cause of Nicholas' death, nor was Frizer ever called to account for it, but then that curling-boy, as you shall hear, inhabited a greyish world outside the clear confines of the law.

As for Shakespeare he never heard at the time of Constable Nicholas' death, and used him later for a clown in a comedy where he gathered his good share of laughs, which may be some consolation for a dagger in the ribs.

\* \* \*

Shakespeare worked hard at the second part of King Harry, and was parted as Lord Scales and I did enact one dead on a battlefield. Most nights he spent working and then he would take the pages he had writ to Marlowe and lived or died by his approval. He feared the hours he had to sit silent whilst Marlowe turned the page, and drank wine, and turned the page, and Shakespeare longed for a smile, or a laugh, or even a frown of disapproval. But at the end of each reading Marlowe said, "Well crowed, little Chanticleer," and brought more wine.

"If you liked not the writing," Shakespeare was so bold once as to say, "would you still say 'Well crowed, Chanticleer' to save yourself trouble?"

"If I liked it not," said Marlowe, "I would give it to Ingram to clean his arse with." At which was Shakespeare greatly reassured.

He showed it to Ned Alleyn who wanted no changes but some hundred lines adding to King Henry's part. And all the others were well-enough pleased, except for Will Slye, who would have Jack Cade more lovable. And when the play was done there were more cheers than ever, and more sweaty nightcaps thrown up, and more chinks taken in. And as for his wages Shakespeare spent them all on buying a supper of plump partridge for Marlowe, where he sat smiling as Marlowe explained to him that to be beloved of the ground-lings was a worse insult than being selected to canonisation, a fate which it seemed unlikely that particular playmaker would ever have to suffer. Meanwhile Frizer grew paler and paler and at the end, vomited into a dish of flummery. Noth-ing at that time, however, could mar Shakespeare's perfect happiness.

So King Harry, like Gaul, was divided into Three Parts, and when he had finished the last page of the last part Shakespeare took the pile of papers in triumph to Marlowe's lodging. He was received by Frizer whose hands seemed covered in a foul and clinging seaweed (the henna with which he was tinting his master's hair). He was put into an outer chamber to wait; and through the chink of a door not quite closed he heard the voices of Master Marlowe and a young man who spoke like a crackle of dry kindling. Standing where he was, Shakespeare could not help but overhear part of their talk. Later he learned that the dry crackle came from a pale young man named Robert Poley, who, I believe, was secretary and secret contriver to that King of secret contrivances, old Sir Francis Walsingham.

"One thing more. The Council have heard also of your words against the Church," Poley was warning.

"It was the wine speaking. Wine has no religion." Marlowe splashed a little as they talked, being naked in a bath tub.

"It seems . . . you see no good in Heaven."

"I love not the thought of it . . . no friends," Marlowe laughed, "and an eternity spent talking to the Archbishop of Canterbury."

"There will be a formal complaint. Their Lordships will summon you." There was a silence, Marlowe was no longer laughing, but Poley reassured him, "There's no great fear, provided you can be trusted in other matters."

"I shall be silent." Now Marlowe sounded serious.

"Do you be."

"Silent!" And then Marlowe laughed again, with a sort of relief. "As the grave, Robert, as the grave."

There was a sound as of a sea creature arising from the waters as Marlowe rose out of his tub and he could be heard shouting to Frizer to go and buy more Rhenish wine. "But not from the Goat, Ingram. The landlady there reverses Christ's miracle and turns the wine into water."

"You can go in now," said Frizer as he passed through the outer room. "I have been sent for wine for you."

So in went Shakespeare and saw Master Poley, pale, expressionless, one of those, as he later said in a rhyme, who are the Lords and Masters of their faces. And Marlowe, wrapped in a sheet like one risen from the tomb, haloed with a tangle of drying, red hair, filled a pipe of tobacco and gave him welcome.

"It is done. Down to the final act!" Shakespeare exulted.

"Rest your play there on the table. Ingram has gone for Rhenish. Tell me, Will. Did you pass Blackfriars on your way?"

"Why, yes." Shakespeare was impatient. He wanted to talk of his death of King Harry and not to prattle of Blackfriars. But Marlowe went on, fascinated by the danger of his speech.

"It was there they hung up the tutor that said a Mass to the boy Earl of Southampton. As they cut him down and opened him up, he sang them a 'Hail Mary'. You can say that for Catholicism, it gives you a good death scene."

There was a big old Bible lying on the littered table and Marlowe went to it, his long pipe stuck between his teeth, and ripped out a page. Then he carried Genesis, Chapter 1, verses 1 to 24 to the fire and lit it for a torch for his pipe.

"A plague on both their Religions." He puffed out with the smoke, "The canting, nose twanging, 'one-clutch-in-the-dark-and-you-roast-in-hellfire' Hypocrisy and the sweet Latin, incense-burning, 'Do-what-you-like-but-pay-the-priest' Hypocrisy. And, whilst the two bludgeon each other to death, do you think a man's soul might creep to freedom, little Chanticleer?" He looked at them both, disappointed at their quiet, "To light tobacco with the Book of Genesis, doesn't that anger you, Master Poley?"

"I'm sorry to disappoint you!" Poley resurrected what might have once been the dead body of a smile.

"Why, there were Indians and Greeks in the world long before your God put down a naked man and woman and then cursed them for an act of natural affection!"

Poley was still smiling as he bowed and went. Marlowe looked sadly at Shakespeare. "Won't you grow angry, Will?"

"I have no time for anger. I want your judgment of my play!" Shakespeare was also prepared to go rather than waste more time upon theology.

"Liar! You want my praise as I want your . . ."

"What, Kit? What do you want from me?"

"Your attention! Listen, rooster! We live, we die. We suffer and they draw the innards out of us. What was your father?"

"A glove-maker in Stratford." He had come for at least two Kings of England. How was his father, Alderman John Shakespeare, concerned in the business?

"Mine was a cobbler in Canterbury. We scramble quickly to the top of the pile as poets and then, they kill us. They will kill you also."

"Me, for what crime?" Now Shakespeare was laughing at him.

"Because they can put no chains on the thoughts of a poet."

And then Frizer came in with the Rhenish and Marlowe looked at the boy as though he were Queen Helen and the Tyrant Tamburlaine all contained in one pale whelp. "Have you no part for Ingram? He plays attendants and minor villains."

Shakespeare looked at Ingram Frizer with less rapture. "Might he not play Bona, sister to the French Queen?"

"He that loves not boys and tobacco is a fool!" So Marlowe sat him down in a cloud of smoke with Ingram beside him, pouring wine and read through Part Three of King Harry with a maddening slowness and then threw it down and there was a lengthy silence Shakespeare feared to break. He looked round the room, at the skulls and horoscopes and silver goblets and Spanish swords and sweet leather-bound books of Horace and Ovid and the perfumes, powders and pomanders and then took courage to say, "Well? Will it do?"

"Your play?" Marlowe sighed. "It is perfect. Truly carpentered. They will cheer and throw up their sweaty nightcaps!"

Shakespeare was smiling, gratified, but Marlowe went on, "Only this ..."

"What?"

"Where are you in your play, Will?"

"I should be there?" Shakespeare was puzzled.

"Surely, as I am Doctor Faustus ... who sold his soul for a moment of idle curiosity! In this whole pile of paper I know not who you are. What do you love?"

"Love?"

"Or hate?"

There was a silence. It was not a question Shakespeare had asked himself. "I love our Theatre."

Marlowe threw back his head, opened his mouth, filled it with Rhenish and laughed at the prentice playmaker. "Tush! Men don't love bare boards and painted faces. Who do you love, other than pot-women?"

Shakespeare was silent, and then I suppose bethought him of the male child whom he had not seen much since the boy was a year old; but he was persuaded he loved Hamnet truly and being persuaded he did, at least, love the Notion of his Son. "I have a boy, a rascal son in Stratford. Him I love, or nothing."

"So the worst you can imagine is . . . What?"

"For a father to kill his son!" Shakespeare ventured.

"It might happen without his knowing, in Civil War, such as these Contentions of the Roses."

"It's not to be imagined!"

"Then must you imagine it! Write me a scene. A father kills an unknown adversary – and when the helmet's off the corpse – behold!"

"His son?"

"And as you write it, think of your rascal. Bring me the scene tomorrow."

Perhaps his prentice days were over, but at these orders Shakespeare began to look angerly. Marlowe continued to give his calm directions. "We shall dine."

"Shall we?"

"At the Inn on Deptford Strand. Kept by a Queen of pot-women. Mistress Bull. I wrote my first couplets to her." Ingram had heated certain irons and Marlowe gave his head to the curling. "Bring me the pages there, then shall I tell if you are a poet, or but a jobbing carpenter."

"I shall not!" Shakespeare was now not a prentice but a shouting playmaker.

Marlowe looked up astonished from beneath the tongs. Meanwhile Shakespeare was launched into an oration. "Am I your hairdresser? Do you command a scene off me, like an ounce of civet or a scented handkerchief? Will you strike your bell and I must crow for you, your little Rooster? I have writ this great pile of paper alone, without your stir. And, while you slept or were at your toilet, I have become the maker of three plays Historical, with one more and a comedy promised. And I am parted with our leading actors, Ned

Alleyn and Burbage. Go order your curling-boy obey you. I am my own poet now!"

"Bring it to me tomorrow at Mistress Bull's," said Marlowe, not the least disturbed by this rebellion.

"I'll not come," and Shakespeare was on his way out of the room.

"I must go out of London, for my health."

Shakespeare stopped and looked back at the curled and healthy poet. "What, are you ill, Lord Vanity?"

"Dying," Marlowe told him. "We are all dying. For poets it comes quicker than for others."

As Shakespeare closed the door he saw Ingram Frizer smiling.

# 7

## Of A Meeting
## At The Inn At Deptford

I HAD IT from my man who was under-servant of Sir Francis
Walsingham that then or thenabouts Ingram Frizer appeared
alone at the house and was received again by the master and
then paid certain monies by one Nick Skeres, who was also in
the service of Sir Francis. What Master Ingram had to report
I know not, nor why one so young and scarcely to be spoken
of among gentlemen should receive more money from that
old devious knight so close to the Counsels of Her Majesty.
But this was an event which occurred.

There also occurred, despite all Shakespeare's rhetoric and
protestations, the writing of the scene in which the father
unwittingly killed his son, and I was eventually parted as the
son. I remember I complained to my mother that I had no
preferment in the company, and only played dead people.
However, I over-run my story for I must tell of the time when
that scene was unplayed and but hot from the pen, and
Shakespeare took it as was planned to the Inn at Deptford
Strand to show his master Marlowe.

Now the Inn was kept by a Mistress Eleanor Bull who was
indeed a pot-woman quite out of the ordinary. She had red
hair and large eyes with small wrinkles of laughter at their
corners, a narrow waist and high bum and bubbies for someone who was surely no longer a girl. She spoke not shrill but
had a gentle and low voice and a memory for those verses
Marlowe read her. He also taught her the nice judgment of a

line and she loved plays as she had once loved a playmaker. In later years Shakespeare would let her behind the arras of the inner stage to hear a play performing. She told me what had passed that day at the Inn at Deptford, although the Coroner's Court did hear another version; but seeing who were their witnesses I am assured that what they heard was as far from the truth as Hell's from Heaven.

It was early in the afternoon that they met at the Deptford Inn, Kit Marlowe, Ingram Frizer, which was natural for where did Marlowe go that Ingram was not with him, Robert Poley and that same Skeres that also served Sir Francis Walsingham. They had been drinking a long time in the garden by the river and it was evening before Marlowe called for the reckoning, so Eleanor Bull went out to him.

There was a low fence which divided off the garden, and the arbour where the party had killed dead dozens of bottles, and the river which flowed below them. Frizer was leaning against this same fence whistling a catch as Marlowe, drunk and garrulous, greeted Mistress Bull in a manner which out-Nedded Alleyn at his most spectacular.

"My Queen!" he cried. "My Zenocrate! The only pot-lady who can judge a couplet and listen to a poet's troubles!" And then he looked into his purse, somewhat rueful. "I have spent a great deal of money!"

"Are you low?" Skeres was grinning at him over the brim of a cup of Rhenish.

Marlowe emptied his purse onto the table and indeed it contained only a little dust and a prodigious quantity of air. "Why, I am quite run out!"

"Even of what you got by telling the Council of the Catholics and the Catholics of the Council?" Poley's dry voice was quiet and he also was smiling.

"Sure, you once had a mass of coin, stamped on both sides." Skeres was speaking loud enough for Mistress Bull to hear.

"Government gold, traitors' gold! Was it all one to you?" Poley asked.

"I had thought to have had enough to entertain you!"

Marlowe seemed puzzled and then, for the first time, Ingram Frizer spoke.

"I shall pay," he said. "For all."

"*You*, Ingram?" Marlowe looked at him incredulous.

"I hate a mean poet!" Frizer called to Mistress Bull, "Give me the reckoning!"

"The world is divided, Ingram," Marlowe smiled, "into the payers and the paid for. Step not out of the part written for you!"

"I pay, I tell you!" Ingram was not to be put off.

"When lambs eat wolves ... then shall Ingram Frizer buy my supper." So said Marlowe and looked as the others threw money down on the table, and at a new great ring glittering on Ingram's finger. "My masters! My rich masters! What have you robbed, Churches or Reputations?" He laughed as he saw Skeres' hand, also ringed, go to his dagger. "What have you sold, live bodies or dead?"

It was then there occurred, well, what occurred exactly? The Coroner's Court brought it in that the three, Frizer, Poley and Skeres, had but acted to defend themselves, and surely Kit Marlowe was a great attacker! But one against three? Mistress Bull saw daggers flash and she is sure now of one thing – when Marlowe's hand held a dagger that same hand was twisted up and back by Frizer, the poet being held by other hands, and his own dagger point was sent plunging at the poet's eye. Then Mistress Bull closed her own eyes and blacked out all the sky, and heard nothing but the sound of her own screams.

*     *     *

When Shakespeare came to that garden with his scene folded in his doublet, the fence was broken. Awash on a landing stage below lay Marlowe's body, and Eleanor Bull was kneeling in the water, cradling him dead. There was a Constable there and others of the Watch. Marlowe's three companions were still standing, watching. The woman looked up, seeing Shakespeare.

"Are you another of them?" she asked.

"He'd have cut us all to ribbons!" Frizer was telling the Constable, and then he looked at the woman with his stony eyes and she confirmed, "They were provoked."

Some of the Watch carried away the body and Mistress Bull was prevailed on to bring strong ale for the Constable. When she had set it down she looked at Shakespeare, and he began to explain himself.

"I was a friend of his from the Theatre, Will ..."

"Master Shagspur?" She had heard of him.

"Shakespeare."

"He called you his Cockerel! You're a poet too, sir?"

"A playmaker."

"Poet, he said. He said you would be the next poet to stand in his shoes, after ... he was gone."

"His shoes. Is that where they stood?" Shakespeare looked at the footmarks, signs of the last scuffle by the water's edge.

"He was a good man, sir." Eleanor Bull sat down. Her eyes were dry, past weeping.

"Better than a good man. He led the way ... we followed him like sheep."

"Well, he's dead." The Constable finished his ale and contemplated calling for another.

It was Ingram Frizer who said, quietly, "Dead Shepherd."

\* \* \*

At Michaelmas came the Great Fair at Southwark, with wire-walkers, stilt-walkers, those who eat fire, giants, monsters, deformed persons, dancing, cock-fights and bear-baiting. Shakespeare was walking through this fair when what should he see but the wool cart from Stratford again and Hamnet Sadler leaping from it with another gift from the countryside. But the press of people was so great he could scarce get at Shakespeare and had to shout at him over sundry heads.

"Hey, Will, from your poor deceived wife. I bring you a fat duck." He managed to throw the bird over the press and Shakespeare caught it.

"Does my poor deceived wife spend all on poultry?"

"I kept your secret, William," Hamnet shouted. "Your good lady knows nothing of your shame as a horse-tender."

Then a great string of dancing citizens passed between them, with some beating drums, other piping flutes. Over this noise and crush Shakespeare yelled his triumph, "You may tell all now, Hamnet. You may tell her the truth."

"Why, it'll break her heart, poor lady!"

"No! Tell her I'll have six silver crowns to send her. And that more pay to see my *Harry the Sixth* than all other pieces. And that Kit Marlowe, being dead, now I am our principal playmaker!"

Hamnet had a moment to look sad at Shakespeare before he was borne away by the throng. He shook his head in despair. "May God forgive you, William Shakespeare," he said. "What terrible lies you do tell!"

So were the two men parted and Shakespeare was alone in the crowd of merrymakers. He turned and saw walking out from between the huge tall legs of a stilt-walker none other than Ingram Frizer, dressed in a velvet suit of Master Marlowe's clothes.

# Part Two

*"Time hath, my lord, a wallet at his
back,
Wherein he puts alms for oblivion."*
Troilus and Cressida

# 8

## *Of My Patron, The Lord Plague*

Now ALL I have writ last night and the night before is safely sewn into the straw of my mattress and I have today gone about my business of polishing candlesticks, cleaning lamps, making lists of known adulterers for special denunciation from the pulpit next Sunday, eating my hunk of cheese in the vestry and sleeping it off in the organ loft. So I am left wondering why, having writ all down of Marlowe's blasphemy and the lechery of players, not to mention the coupling of men and boys and poets and pot-girls, I am not struck down by a thunderbolt, or changed into a pillar of salt, or at least visited by the Great Sickness which was held to be the wages of all sin when I was a child, although I did notice that the good died of it as well as the wicked and it brought as quick an end in the Bishop's Palace as it did in the brothel.

And this brings me to the Great Character who plays so large a part in this History, namely Master Death, or if you would be more particular, my Lord Plague, whose patronage gave me my start in the Theatre, and in contest with whom Will Shakespeare wrote some of his most Notable Verses.

I was then, I suppose, fourteen or fifteen; it seems so long ago I wonder this old hand that writes this is still the hand that did scrub the stage, feel for coins in others' pockets and grope for his first pot-girl. I noticed it at first among the rats I slept with, how some grew sleepy and then died. I had not to give these same rats a Christian burial, for to be sure their friends and relatives had them for dinner. And then we heard of neighbours, friends, strangers, all sorts and conditions of rogues and honest men, light women and sainted sisters, who were taken hold of by the Great Sickness, kissed upon the lips by his Plaguey Lordship and left within a fortnight to travel by cart to an open tip with a shovelful of lime for company.

Now the way of it was this. The first they noticed was a swelling under the armpit or oxter, then came a heating, to boiling almost, of the blood, then a sickness and a vomiting, then a restlessness, then a listlessness, then a chilling, then a sleepfulness and finally all those kissed or smitten left home on the short journey to the pit and the long problematical journey beyond.

Once a house had one in it sick of the plague, why then it was boarded up and none, sick or well, let to come out of it, for fear of carrying the infection. So would you pass those houses marked with a blue mark, and from within you might hear the pitiful cries and knocking of those imprisoned, with no escape unless they were rich enough to bribe a Constable.

Now it is true that the streets around Cripplegate and Shoreditch were none too cleanly, being crammed with Dicing Houses, Brothel Houses, Bowling Alleys and other Disorderly Places. The narrow alleys, being too small for traffic, became tips for excrements, graveyards for dogs, cats and even horses. There was offal from the slaughter houses left in clogged gutters, and from such pestilential air as was there given off it might be that my Lord Plague had his generation. But the common opinion was, you got it from the drinking water.

Of course many said it also came by fornication, and many an excellent night of merry couplement was lost because of the fear of the intervention of His Lordship. Some vowed it was due to eating onions, or wearing new linen, or being out in rain or wet weather, or paring the finger nails, or some thought it came from swearing or blaspheming or not stifling a fart. One man in Moorgate refused to breathe in lest he take the infection, and was dead within five minutes. But many who ate onions, blasphemed, walked through rain, pared their nails, released their farts and fornicated, lived on to boast of their good fortune.

However, I cannot say that in the Plague Year we were especially doleful. As a man grows used to living with a scold, or the lack of a leg, or any other disability, so the daily prospect of death grew to be something ordinary. Indeed, there was a certain gaiety to be derived from wondering who went next, and as I recall the music seemed louder in that year, the capering and dancing more energetic and the laughter longer, for truly a man needs must laugh at a joke if it's the last he'll ever hear.

We moved at that time from the Rose, forsaking Ned Alleyn, to take our plays and players over to Shoreditch, to an old Theatre which had been built by Dick Burbage's father Jack, who had been a joiner and then became a play-actor. It had something fallen out of repair when we moved into it; but it was a time of excitement for us. Whereas we had all been bond-slaves of Ned Alleyn at the Rose, at the Theatre the actors were to have shares, they contributed their savings for fresh paint and new tirings. Shakespeare's contribution was to be a new Tragical Historical of Crookback Dick, the Third Richard; although this play seemed to take as long in birth as a whore's child when the mother pleads the state of her belly so she may not hang.

So we were crossing the town to Shoreditch with Richard's throne (if he should ever be writ) and the Old King's coffin (if his funeral scene should ever come to birth). William Bell, who was a great drinker of small breakfast ale all day long, had a barrel carried with him and drank as we travelled. We were not much dashed in spirits as we passed the dead carts and their melancholy loads. Will Bell called out at the travellers in the carts that they should be of good cheer as, being dead, they need fear death no longer.

I was thinking of one thing only, who should play the Lady Anne whom Crookback wooed across her dead husband's coffin in a scene I knew Will Shakespeare had in head if not yet on paper. I knew that long ninny Alex Cooke was chosen for the part; but he was too old, and not really pretty. I sat in the back of the actors' cart as we passed the load of corpses. My doublet was out at elbow as my breeches were out at arse, my shoes leaked water like a sieve and I was chewing on a crust of stale bread as all our money was gone in shares in the new enterprise; and all I wanted was to be a fair, spirited Lady and England's Queen.

So I was thinking when we jerked to a stop in the Theatre and we were out, pulling thrones, pushing coffins, pouring small ale, and my mother was guarding with her life a work she had just begun, a plaited wicker-work hump for the back of that ill-shapen but as yet unwritten Monarch, Dick the Third.

When I was out I turned a cartwheel on the stage and stared at my black hands. "This stage is dirty," I complained to Burbage and knew at once what the answer would be. "Then you shall scrub it, little Jack Rice!" William Bell took two more cups of ale and Christened the stage with vomit to add interest to my part. Some of the old boards needed fastening and the whole wanted for a coat of paint (another role I was promised) but we were well content with our new house.

"May we have long years here my masters," Burbage called to us to silence and Bell poured more ale for a toast. "And many plays brought to a happy life!"

It was then we heard a great bell tolling. They had a burial pit in Finsbury Fields, just outside the wall of the Theatre. We all fell silent for a moment, listening, and then Burbage bade us set to and tighten the stage planks, else he would squeak to a soliloquy.

# 9

## Of Hal The Horse-Thief,
## Doctor Alcibiades' Man

WITH THE GREAT SICKNESS there came no lack of curers.
Doctors and Apothecaries flourished as did Mountebanks and
Magicians. One day the actors were assembled in the Dagger
Inn in Holborn, as usual discussing the Great Feast they
would have if only Shakespeare's play were writ and the
Theatre open again and successful: and I, who had heard this
repeated a dozen times each day and more on Sundays, and
was weary of a diet of hope and water, went out to steal an
apple from a fruit cart and in the street heard a mountebank
in a tall hat and star-spangled robe harangue a gullible group
of sturdy citizens. At this mountebank's side, holding a tray
of ordinary pebbles and dressed in an old leather doublet and
darned hose was a personable young man I came to know
better as Hal the Horse-thief.

"What do you fear?" cried Dr. Alcibiades to those who
would listen. "Do you fear plague? The swelling under the
armpit or oxter? The gut-griping ruptures? The vomiting of
the spleen? The grey-green corruption of the flesh? The lime-
kiln in the mouth? The fire in the belly? The wateriness of
the knees? The sword-thrust in the privates? The ice cold
palsies in the bones? Do you fear Death?" His voice sank to a
whisper and then he shouted triumphantly, "I, Doctor
Alcibiades. That was once physician to the Queen of Egypt!
I am come with my man Hal ... Who is privy to my
mysteries ... To banish fear. I tell you, Masters. They have no

plague in Egypt! Because the stones of Egypt do drive all
sweats and foul diseases out of the body. Hold up the basket,
Hal! Here we have stones, from the Pyramids of Egypt."

Hal the Horse-thief now began to sell, to my amazement,
his poor basket of pebbles to the crowd and did a roaring
trade, as the learned Doctor continued, "Do but grasp one
such stone and all sickness will be drawn out of you for ever!
And for this sweet health! For this surety of life I ask, not
guineas, Gentles, not sovereigns, not angels, not half angels
either. Put out crowns only, my friends. My man Hal passes
among you with the Pyramids of Egypt!"

When most of the stones were sold, Doctor Alcibiades bade
his patients but close their eyes, clutch their part of the
pyramids and think of Queen Cleopatra (a thought more like
to raise their pricks than flatten their bubucles). And of
course, as I had suspected, when all eyes were closed the man
Hal proved himself to be no more than a common Nip or
Foist and passed among the citizens and cut no less than four
purses with a sharp dagger.

"Breathe out slowly," intoned Doctor Alcibiades, "so you
may feel all the sickness leaving you." But one fat burgher
also feeling his heavy purse leaving him, opened his eyes and
cried, "Stop thief! A Constable! Call out the Watch!"

So Doctor Alcibiades swiftly turned his cloak inside out
and, habited now like Master Parson, started a Sermon and
Hal was away, helter-skelter down a narrow alley with half
the Pyramids of Egypt being flung after him. I took a sharp
turn, met him halfway down the alley and pointed him to the
back door of the Dagger Inn, into which he dived for refuge,
leaving me a whole silver crown in my dirty palm for my
trouble. When the citizens came running up I pointed them
in the other direction.

*     *     *

In the Dagger I found the hungry actors were sat round,
watching crisp capons and plump partridges being sent to
other customers, and pulling out their last coins for a sword,

a cloak, a pound of gunpowder for the cannons, or a small cheese to keep them alive till the play was given. They had a hat on the table into which each flung his groat, his penny or his florin and when it came to Shakespeare's turn he vowed he had no money, but threw in instead a pile of parts and papers, "The Tragical History of King Richard the Third, with a full account of the Abominable Murder of the Princes in the Tower and the Drowning, Head over Heels in A Malmsey Butt, of the Great Duke of Clarence".

"Finished, Will?" Burbage couldn't believe it.

"Down to his most deserved Death!"

And, as the actors were applauding, a young man rushed up to them, grabbed up the hat, scattered its contents, clapped it on his head and started as if they had been talking together all afternoon.

"Now, gentlemen. What were we discussing?"

"Nothing with you!" Will Kempe looked at him amazed.

"Say I was with you and I'll buy you wine!" And he dropped a gold coin on the table which the actors looked at as though it were the miracle of the loaves and the fishes. "Burgundy Wine for you, gentlemen, if you don't betray me. You there! Pot-girl!"

"Coming, Master." Kate was the colour of a dirty blanket that day, and crouched by the fire shivering, although her fingers almost touched the logs. She dragged herself over to the actors, who greeted her with the usual tired and tawdry jests.

"A kiss, Kate!" cried Burbage. "For King Richard the Third!"

"William the First is before Richard the Third," Shakespeare had his arm about her. "Why, Kate. You're shivering!"

"My arm's that sore, lugging pots for actors."

"And doing other services for playmakers!" Will Kempe laughed at her. "Lie with me, sweet Kate! A dancer is more athletical than a poet!"

"Lie with you? I'd rather lie in my grave!" When she had received our orders for Burgundy wine and Cheeses Burbage looked at Hal, the host.

"What *are* you?" he asked him.

"I am Hal the Horse-thief, servant to the Great Doctor Alcibiades," Hal answered from under his hat. "We have cures for gut-grip, the Bots, fire in the belly and the corruption of the privates. Also we cure Plague." With which he pulls out one of his precious pebbles. "You hold this in your hand and laugh in the face of Death. It comes from the Pyramids of Egypt!"

"Looks like a lump from the Pyramids of Cheapside." Fat William Bell was not greatly convinced.

"Don't try and cheat us, boy!" Will Kempe warned and Shakespeare added, "You won't fool us by make-believe. That's our business."

"Why, are you thieves?" Hal peered at the company from under his hat with respect.

"No. We are actors," Shakespeare told him.

"Actors!" Hal looked at Shakespeare. "What do you play? The Fool?"

"No, fool, I am the poet."

"More fool you. What riches is in poetry?"

Burbage, warmed by the prospect of good wine, rebuked him, "Will Shakespeare will give you a golden line. Which may outlast the life of mortals."

"Like the Pyramids of Egypt!" Hal laughed at him. And then Kate came up to the table, greenish now rather than grey, slopping a jug of wine. She stumbled, sick and giddy, and Hal was up, holding her as she near fainted away. He called on us to help her, but before we could move, the front door of the Dagger burst open, Hal pulled down the brim of our communal hat, and there were two Constables in the midst of us.

"We seek a rogue pedlar and a Mountebank," said one. "A fraudsman selling Egyptian stones, as a cure for the Great Sickness."

The Constables stared at us, and we were all silent, whether from love of Hal's gold coins, or respect for a fellow performer, or from that natural enmity which must ever divide actors from Constables of the Watch, I know not. Then Hal spoke in a curious high voice from under the hat.

"Help me, Masters! There is one here sick of the plague."
Which was enough to send the two Constables scuttling out,
holding their breaths, with their eyes popping like fishes.

When they had gone Shakespeare laughed. "The plague!
That was a good counterfeit." But now Hal the Horse-thief
had his hand under Kate's arm and was restoring her to her
chair by the fire.

"That was no counterfeit," he said. "She's swollen under
the arm. Sit still, girl. You'll draw no more ale!"

At which the actors began to shuffle towards the door, with
little Jack Rice not lagging behind either. But Kate was looking at Shakespeare and she said, in a voice most pathetic,
"Will! Goodbye, sweet Will!"

Hal smiled at Shakespeare. "Will you not kiss her goodbye?
You can only die for it!"

Kate's eyes were full of that tender request and she whispered, "Please, Will." But he stood as if stone, and came not
near her.

"Are you afraid?" Hal asked him.

"Perhaps."

"Why, courage then!" Hal was mocking him now and,
most unexpectedly, threw a couple of his own verses in his
teeth. "What cannot be avoided, 'Twere childish weakness to
lament or fear.' I know your verses by heart, Will Shakespeare. I cannot keep my foot out of brothels, theatres and
other men's houses while they sleep at nights. Come. I'll
throw dice with you." And at that he leaned down and kissed
dying Kate full on the lips. Then he looked up at Shakespeare
as if challenging him to a throw.

He had a theatre to open and a new play. He had no time
for dying. Shakespeare turned and went out of the door and
we actors with him. He never saw Kate again, and I know
now why it seemed that Hal the Horse-thief had chosen to
play a game with him, and undoubtedly won.

# 10

## *In Which Shakespeare Becomes a Barnard And Breaks Into A Fine Lord's Dwelling*

A DAY OR TWO after his first meeting with Hal, no doubt reproving himself for his churlish manner to Kate the pot-girl if indeed she were taken of the Great Sickness, and conscious of his poor showing in the matter, Shakespeare returned to the Dagger, which he found duly barred and bolted with a Blue Cross on the door. He was rattling hopelessly, with some thought that his pot-girl was trapped within and might be rescued, when he was hailed from the other side of the street.

"Closed!" Hal was sitting on a wall, trimming his nails with a dagger. "Her Majesty's Council is concerned to keep us alive. Strange, seeing how many of us are hanged up by their Order." He slid off the wall and strolled across to Shakespeare. "Do you want to kiss your pot-girl now?"

"Is she taken?" Shakespeare looked sadly at the barred door, and felt the silence of that once busy Inn.

"Oh, yes, she is taken. You have missed your chances. Drink a little with me?"

"I have business . . ."

"None that is as urgent as gaining courage, and forgetting how you left her. Brandy wine's the medicine."

"I never had Brandy," said Shakespeare. It was true, he never had.

"I'll take you to the Wise Virgin . . . No . . . Better, to enlarge your experience, I'll take you to the Jolly Struggler!"

Whether Shakespeare was tempted by the Brandy, or by that curious mystery, his new companion, or even by a loathing of the white page waiting him back at the Theatre I know not, but he went to the Jolly Struggler, which was a pit for wrestlers and a drinking den also, much frequented by light rogues and heavy Bawkers from the bowling alleys, Draw latches, Rufflers, Priggers, Ephesians who did swagger, rob and bully, Catchers and Shifters who sold brass for gold, or kindling wood for relics of the One True Cross, and Abraham's men who feigned madness and begged at street corners. There was also in there a fine crowd of Tinkers and Robbers with their Doxies, and some rare Egyptians or Moonmen of the Romany family from whom I have the honour to trace some of my descent.

Hal led Shakespeare down the lanes and alleys to this place, and as he passed the doors marked with a Blue Cross he said he found the plague a better gamble than the game of Primero at cards, for who knew what they would draw next, the Hangman or the Coffin. And then he knocked on the door of the Struggler and it was opened a chink by one "Iron Neck" Barnaby, so called because he had been cut down after ten minutes swinging and lived to tell of it. Seeing Hal, Barnaby opened wide, as if to a person of some honour in that Community.

Now Will Shakespeare had some acquaintance of rogues, and may have once lodged in a nest of Anglers (those who steal at night with long hooked staves) in the years he lay fallow, but truly he had never seen such a company as Hal there acquainted him with. Indeed he saw some of the Great Lords Spiritual and Temporal of the Midnight Society, together with their Mogs or Doxies, including the "Upright Man" who controlled all Foists and initiated them into their Mystery by pouring a quart pot of ale over their heads and telling them that from henceforth it should be lawful for them to thieve.

So, as the half-stripped wrestlers struggled in the pit, and bets were won or lost as bones creaked or snapped and sweaty bodies were tossed like pillows, a great number of Brandy tots were emptied. Shakespeare attended to all Hal told him as close as if he were reading his Plutarch or his Holinshed for tales to furnish out his playmaking. Hal explained how the "Gripe" will lay bets on the wrestling, the result of which was as certain as that by next year half the company would be hanged, to cull the innocent "Vincent", or fool, out of his money. And as a final sign of Honour there came to sit with them for an hour she who reigned over England, Moll Cutpurse, who could roar and fight with her sword strong as a man, and who showed them her long first and middle fingers which made her as Foist of purses and pockets *non pareil*.

"Is it true, you never tasted Brandy wine before?"

Shakespeare was staring into the corner where an old fat fellow of faded gentility was listening to a ragged, ruffianly Captain boast of his great daring in the Wars. Snatches of their talk came to him through the haze of Hal's Brandy, and he answered vaguely, "No, truly."

"Not at a Lord's table, Will? Have you no great courtier to be your patron?"

"Poor Kit Marlowe had friends at Court. The last I saw of him his brain was full of dagger." Shakespeare's Brandy pot was empty and Hal had it filled again. The golden mists swirled about him, and through them Shakespeare saw Hal's eyes staring.

"But if you had a fine Earl for a friend," the voice sounded far away and much amused, "you might sleep in his silk sheets and leave the window open."

"Why leave the window open?" Another gulp of Brandy went down, cool and no longer fiery.

"So I could cant his house and foist his silver candlesticks." For no special reason Shakespeare began to find this exquisitely humorous; he started laughing. But Hal was perfectly serious.

"Have you never canted a house, Will?"

"Never."

"Not even acted as a Barnard?"

"A Barnard? What's that?"

"You would write plays! You would seek to entertain

decent thieves and cutpurses! And you ask what a Barnard is? Why, you'll ask me what a Jenkin is next."

"Then I'll ask you. What is a Jenkin?"

"The Jenkin opens the window of the crib, with the point of his dagger. And the Barnard keeps watch. Then the Jenkin brings out the candlesticks, and straight with them to the Peter!"

"Who's the Peter?"

"Who's the Peter! Him that sells them to the John. I know. Who's the John?"

"Right. Who?"

"Why, such as you, Will Shakespeare. The fool in the market place, who buys stolen property! What ignorance! You sit in that old Theatre filling your head with dusty Histories, and know nothing of the fine art of rogues and pickpockets. True, all poets are cowards. You most of all."

"I have not been brave especially. I live in daily fear of our play not pleasing." After the playing of his three parts of the Sixth Harry, some dirty, ragged-bearded wit out of the University whose name now eludes my memory, had attacked Will as an upstart crow, beautified with others' feathers, a Johannes factotum aping the excellence of better poets. This pamphlet had dug its dagger into him and left a wound that ached in apprehension whenever he had a new play in head. Was he but an ape? A crow disguised? A mimicking servant of greater models? He took another gulp of Brandy and banished the notion.

"And if your play displeases, will they hang you at Tyburn?"

"No," Shakespeare was laughing again, "but it will feel the same."

"Come!" Hal's voice was sharp now, like a man calling hounds together. "You tremble at death and fear life also. You fear to kiss your mistress goodbye or even act Barnard, a part with not a risk attached."

"Do you say so? Damn you! I'll be your Barnard!"

"Tonight! Southampton House here in Holborn is empty. The young Lord is away in the country and there is no guard but an old stooping watchman, always drunk. More Brandy, poet. It may give you an ounce of courage."

Shakespeare has talked to me of why, in the name of Sanity and All Good Sense, he, a playmaker with a new Theatre to fill and golden opinions still to be won, wanted to act Barnard on such a perilous and foolish undertaking. He had not shown himself brave on the occasion of sweet Kate's last "goodnight" and there entered perhaps, into his Brandy-fumed brain, some thought of paying for that craven moment with a foolhardy act, a gamble with his life that had no point or purpose in it. And then this Hal seemed now so strange and unaccountable. In his very youth, in his good cheer in the face of danger and his authority, there was some mystery, and Shakespeare would get to the heart of it. But stronger than all he thought was the distilled French essence of the Brandy wine, which set his legs staggering as Hal held his "Barnard" upright and on a straight course towards their canting knavery.

It was dark night when they came to the great house which, it is true, had a wall around it, but in that wall there was a little postern gate which had been left swinging open.

"Blessed be Saint Agatha," Hal said. "Patron of all thieving rogues and Jenkins." So they staggered across a dark grassy patch and were soon against a huge tall window where Hal had his dagger out and was gently tickling the lock in order to cant his crib. At which moment there came the great baying of hounds, and Shakespeare had a fleeting sight of black shapes, sharp teeth and lolling tongues before Hal, his Upright Man and Rogue Master, having got the window open, took the poet by the neck and hauled him in at the window, saying that he best hurry unless he wished to make meat for the kennels.

So Shakespeare found himself in the dark, half drunk, in a Great Lord's house where he had no business to be.

"So I have promoted you," Hal whispered. "Now you are a Jenkin; welcome to the tribe!" At which the whole world then seemed to blaze with light and Shakespeare's heart leaped straight up to his mouth and stayed there for the next

ten minutes, for as he looked he saw they were surrounded
by a crowd of Sturdy Rascals (servants, in truth, of the place)
in nightshirts each carrying a blazing torch, or a branched
candlestick, and each armed with a staff, or a sword, or a
stout poker. Leader of this band appeared to be a tiny page,
a very nimble imp, in nightcap and gown, who held, deliberately pointed, a loaded blunderbuss at least as long as he.

"Well, what a crib is this!" Hal looked round at the fine
hangings of tapestries, at the silver-chased goblets and golden
standing-bowls, the chests and chairs and presses, all of carved
walnut and rosewood with fine in-lay, the Turkey-work
carpets and treble-stitched cushions. "We have fallen on luck.
Here, you men!" (He shouted at the grim faces surrounding
them.) "This is William Shakespeare!"

"Ssh!" Shakespeare was desperate. "Tell them not our
names!"

"William Shakespeare!" Hal went on even louder. "The
Great Poet and Supreme Barnard!"

"Shall we run?" Shakespeare whispered again, with a longing look at the open window behind them.

"Run? What, and leave all this treasure? Here, boy!" Hal
shouted at a tall, night-shirted figure. "Hand Master William
Shakespeare that candlestick!"

To his great amazement Shakespeare found the silver
branched candlestick put into his hand, where it trembled
like a drab leaf in an Autumn wind.

The boy with the blunderbuss now spoke in a high treble,
"What do you want?"

"Want?" Hal was thoughtful. "Want? I think ..." His
voice changed, it sounded easy, almost gentle but with a flint
edge to it, the voice of one born easily to command. "I think
I want, a dish of plover's eggs and a cool bottle of the
Bavarian White."

Thus did Henry Wriothesley (said as Risely) Third Earl of
Southampton and Baron Titchfield in the Peerage of England,
otherwise known as Hal the Horse-thief, man to that Great
Quack and Mountebank Doctor Alcibiades, entice William
Shakespeare into his home.

# 11

## *Of How Will Shakespeare Found And Left A Patron*

PLOVER'S EGGS AND Bavarian White were not enough to replace Shakespeare's strength after such an Amazing Conclusion to so Perilous an Adventure. He sat by a great fire of perfumed logs, opposite a fair youth who was some nine and a half years younger than he, for Hal, as I shall still call him now though we know him to be the Lord Hal, the Noble Harry, heir to two houses, one hundred and fifty servants, numerous horses, farms, parks and pleasances, together with all manner of jewels and fine furnishings, was then but nineteen years old. So having taken off his old leather jacket and horse-thief's hose, being now arrayed in a furred, velvet gown and slippers worked in gold, how did the Lord Harry look to Shakespeare? Why, as one whose features were long and delicate, whose eyes were deep as pools, but yet as pools in which the water could be ice-cold for the diver, whose lips were full and the corners of whose mouth could show amusement and sudden contempt, whose chestnut hair fell longer at one side of his head, whose fingers were tapering, whose body was slim as a girl's and perfectly trained in all exercise of riding, leaping, or playing with the foils. In short, one who had that beauty which Shakespeare, for all his gifts and capabilities, must live without, and, having it not, he admired it above all else and there was little he could refuse it.

And as for Hal he was still laughing as to the way he had gulled Shakespeare; but he comforted him by the following dinner, served by his young page, a pocket imp whom he named "Hercules" and by the tall footman who, being apparently nameless, was called none other than the "Tall Footman". Many years later Shakespeare remembered that first dinner, all of which must have been kept simmering in the great kitchens of Southampton House against his Lordship returning from Foisting, Nipping, Robarding or Bowsing in a Thieves' Kitchen. There were dishes of butter, oysters, a leg of mutton, a loin of veal, venison pasty, a rabbit, partridges, two whitings, a side of green fish, strawberries, cherries, cream, musk confects and violet confects with oranges, lemons and cream and lettuce for salad. At last Hercules brought in a Spanish galleon of spun sugar floating in a sea of claret, and as they bombarded it with walnuts so it sank and so once more was England saved. With this they emptied three pints of white wine and four of red, and with more Brandy-wine the evening passed into that state of dream from which it had never gone far.

"I have lacked for something," Hal said as they staggered together up the great marble stair with Hercules holding a small candle before them, "since they hung Charles my poor tutor for saying a Mass."

"Someone to entertain you?"

"No. Rather someone to love."

Next morning Shakespeare woke to the cries of peacocks in the trees of that garden near Holborn in which Southampton House was situate. Against his cheek he felt the cool caress of spun silken sheets. He lay a little remembering the rough kiss of a straw bed when he tended horses outside the old Rose Theatre.

\*　　\*　　\*

Now what can I tell you of Hal, or the Lord Harry, who was not contented with the Humble Station in which God had thought fit to place him, that of an Earl and a Baron in the English Peerage, but sought to better himself by becoming a Thief and a Jenkin or even aimed higher at the very position of Upright Man, Master and Convener of Foists?

Hal's grandfather had been plain Thomas Wriothesley, who was a cunning lawyer and servant to that old mountain of lechery and bag of diseases the Eighth Harry. (Come in, Rector, have a look at this, all you Parish Councillors and Parliament men, for I am abusing a King, which is about the only permitted subject I have yet tackled in these pages.) Indeed he so helped that fat and fornicating Monarch despoil monasteries, empty convents and annex Abbeys that he not only enriched the King, but himself acquired Titchfield, a fair house in the County of Hants, once he had driven the Abbot and diverse idle and lecherous monks from its fair towers, lawns, ice houses and fish ponds. Old Thomas, who became first Earl of Southampton, was zealous in the burning of Lutheran heretics, and it's said worked the wheel of the rack himself when some pious woman was for questioning; but he loved poetry, spent much in the endowment of Universities and, for some reason which is not to be readily understood, wept real tears on the death of the Eighth King Harry.

Thomas's son, the second Earl, was a bird of a different feather. He was fixed very deep into his Catholic faith, and, as I have noted with many who spent much time in the company of God, it became difficult for men to live with him, and women also, for his wife, who, though devout, found not much sport in the constant conning of missals and rattling of beads, preferred to do her rattling with a "common" person named Donnesame. So the marriage of Hal's mother and father was scarce happy, and not improved by the second Earl's spending some years in the Tower for his Catholic adherence. Neither did he please those in power by complaining of the bill presented to him for his lodging by the Lord Lieutenant of that gloomy edifice on his release; although this bill, they say, contained only double the fair charge for wine and meats incurred, something having to be set aside to feed the Ravens.

When our Hal was six years old his light and straying mother bade him take a letter to his gloomy father in which she protested that she knew no more of Donnesame than

might be seen betwixt his hat and his doublet. It seems Hal
liked not this task, for his father scrumpled the letter and
threw it among a litter of puppies in a corner of the chamber.
From then on Hal never trusted women, nor perhaps liked
them much, though he tumbled his share, and one in particular you shall hear of, and got Mistress Vernon with child
and had to make her his Countess. But whilst his father lived
he was, after the occasion of the letter, forbade to see his
mother, and spent his time with priests and tutors, farm boys
and huntsmen, and those lads that did tend the hawks or
make music after dinner at Titchfield.

Hal's father died when he was almost eight, and the boy
was then a Royal Ward put in the care of the Great Master
Secretary Burghley, the older Cecil, by whom he was well
schooled in French, Latin, Dancing, Writing, Drawing and
Cosmography or the Art of Charting the Heavens. At Cecil's
house he met and worshipped Robert Devereux, Earl of
Essex, who could ride, leap, fence and run at a tilt so that at
fifteen he seemed to be a God. And they both laughed at and
teased little hunchback Robert Cecil, then nineteen and pale
from book-reading, who would become Master Secretary
Cecil and have his part to play in the condemning of both
Earls Essex and Southampton to be disembowelled in public.

Hal was but twelve when Essex went to fight in the Low
Countries and at fourteen he was still too young to board an
English ship to grapple and put to flight the Great Armada.
Without doubt he missed such dangers in his life, so when
he had finished with Cambridge and become a learned,
dicing, duelling, swaggering, drinking, swearing, frisking and
fornicating student at the Inns of Court, he found in Taverns
and thieving the dangers he had missed on the battlefield,
and the enjoyable risk of dying at the end of a rope was the
best he could do for lack of an Enemy's cavalry assault or
naval cannonade.

At the time when he lured Will Shakespeare into his house
Hal was in something of a disfavour with his guardian for his
reluctance to marry Burghley's grand-daughter, one Lady
Elizabeth Vere, a pale girl whom Hal swore he loved as much

as he did thin gruel or a cold warming pan. Like his father
he kept more servants than he could afford, but he also drank
more wine than was good for him, quarrelled easily, loved
lightly and got great pleasure in his attendance at the Court
of England's Queen one day and at Moll Cutpurse's the next.

One other matter. Hal's father had erected a huge tomb
in Titchfield Church in which he lay among statues, por-
traitures and Armours with the kneeling child Hal carved
mourning. So Hal was for ever planning his own additions to
the sepulchre, seeming to fear above all else that his life
might pass unnoticed to future generations. Now whether he
brought Will Shakespeare into his house for a friend, a lover
or a tomb-maker I cannot be sure; but it may be that he
intended to use him as all three.

"How many of your actors wake to silk sheets and the cry
of peacocks?" Hal asked Will, rousing him.

"They wake to straw, and sour beer, most of them."

Then Hercules brought a dish of pheasants cold with hot
bread, eggs buttered and white wine from Bavaria, and later
a big silver ewer of Rose Water to wash the poet's hands and
face and feet, which were dried on a napkin of fine linen.

*     *     *

So for three days and nights we saw not Will Shakespeare.
My mother was plaiting away at the hump for King Richard,
and I was contriving a thousand ways in which I might get
the part of Queen Anne out of the desperate grasp of Alex
Cooke, including, I fear me, such wild plans as denouncing
him for a secret addict of the Mass or dropping the thunder-
sheet on his head as he passed under the tower. I even put a
spell on him I bought for a penny off Doctor Alcibiades,
whom I saw now playing the part of a legless beggar on the
steps of St. Margaret's in Blackfriars, but the spell only
seemed to make the Vile Cooke more sprightly, his eye
glittered and the canting hypocrite took to chasing pot-girls.

"Make haste with that hump," I told mother late one night,
when she was up working. "Burbage has Richard's crown

and Richard's wig and Richard's cloak. He lacks only Richard's Crouched Back."

"I'm plaiting as quickly as I can!" she said wearily. "Only my old arm grows tired and I'm hungry. I dream all the while of a dish of calf's foot and boiled turnip, or a rabbit with a pig's petty toes."

"You shall have pig's petty toes for breakfast daily," I told mother, "when Burbage parts me as Queen Anne and I am paid for as a leading actor."

"Alex Cooke is parted as the Queen of England, and you, Jack, are to be a dead body in the Field of Bosworth. I would eat a round of cheese had we but the money for it."

At which I showed her the coin Lord Hal had tossed to me when I showed him the back entrance of the Dagger. "Have you been a bad lad, Jack?" she asked me, and when I denied it she, being a loyal member of the family of actors, insisted that I give it to Dick Burbage for the play. Of course I agreed to do so, but when I next saw Burbage the coin had mysteriously vanished. I told mother it was her fault. She had not well sewn up my pocket.

That night she started to shiver and her teeth chattered, and towards dawn she grew hot and vomited. She had an ache under her arm and could scarce lift it to finish plaiting of the hump.

\*   \*   \*

Meanwhile Hal and Will Shakespeare played games and went not out of the gate of Southampton House. They played at Cards, Tables, Dice, Shovelboard, Chess-play, Small Trunks, Shuttlecock, Billiards and Tennis. They played at the Foils and Hal showed his friend how to hold his left hand up like a gentleman and, penetrating Will's penetrable guard, scored a soft hit with the buttoned foil, just under the poet's heart.

They played at Primero and French Ruff and a sort of game of naval battle, pushing silver galleons about on a table, with long poles. They played at Irish, Lurch and Tick Tack, and at almost all the games was the Earl of Southampton victorious.

"I would I had a poet," Hal said, as they played at Ninepins in the garden.

"What for?"

"To entertain me. To make me laugh, and make me Immortal." Hal threw a ball which swung and bounced and sent eight pins flying, one of them Hercules had to retrieve from a pond where it floated among lilies and golden carp.

"Come with me to Titchfield," Hal said as they lay on a bank of sweet herbs, resting after tennis. "We will spend our days in hunting, hawking or tickling trout in the streams. And after dinner we shall sit in front of the logs in the great library and you shall write such verses as shall make me deathless!"

"What, will verses save you from Lord Ague, the shroud and the marble tomb?"

"If I get your verses, then I shall live as long as you are remembered."

"I shall not be remembered long" – Shakespeare stood up – "if I do not see my third King Richard acted."

"That old Chronicle!" Hal yawned, he cared only for the First Part of King Hal of Southampton, with a full account of his Great Talents, Personal Beauty and Claim to Undying Fame. "I thought you had that writ."

"Why, so I have. Now it must be played."

"Then let the actors play it."

"You forget me, Hal. I am an actor."

"Why so you are." Hal looked at him, his eyelids drooped against the sun. "For a moment I thought you had been a person."

After dinner (all fish, halibuts, more oysters, plaices, whitings, congers and a huge eel pie with pastry shaped like the Tower of London) Shakespeare said, "I must go tomorrow."

"To your dull wife at Stratford, little shopkeeper?"

"To the Theatre. To my true family."

"So. I am not your family?"

"No."

"What am I then?"

"My friend. I hope you are my friend."

Hal was not pleased at this talk of going. His hand as he raised his glass of white Bavarian shook a little in anger. "I had tried," he said, "to be your tutor."

"Why, what did you teach me?"

"How to fence and play at tennis. How to eat oysters without getting your cuffs wet. How to drink without getting grease from your lips on the rim of the glass. How to wear your cloak like a gentleman, and how to bathe your feet daily. I was also teaching you something of love. It's a lesson you won't learn from actors."

"However, I must go back to them."

"I have not made you comfortable?"

"Indeed. But I cannot sell Dick Burbage and the others for a dish of plover's eggs."

"What if I ordered you to stay?"

"Save your breath. You do not command me or my verses yet."

"You will come back?"

"I do not think so. Our worlds are far apart."

Hal struck on a bell and Hercules came in bowing. "Show Master Shakespeare out by the servants' entrance," he said. "It seems that is what he prefers."

So Will Shakespeare made his bow and left, wondering if he would ever sleep in silk sheets or be woken by peacocks again.

# 12

## *Of How Mother Won Me A Part*

WHEN SHAKESPEARE CAME back to us he found mother sick,
lying on a bed of sacks and cloths in a corner of the tiring
room. The hump was finished, and she was very tired.

"You never knew what trouble you gave," she said to him,
"when you took to writing a hunchback."

"What ails her?" Shakespeare looked round at the other
actors.

"A rheum, perhaps," said Alex Cooke, who was ever in the
wrong.

"A guts ache?" Will Kempe suggested.

"A guts ache brought about by fasting?" Bell doubted it.

Shakespeare asked her to raise her arm, but the movement
pained her. "It's old bones," she gasped, "and all that plaiting." There was a silence in the tiring room, and then Burbage
called them all out to a rehearsal.

When they were gone mother called me to bring the old
handkerchief, the one that had been worked by my Egyptian
grandmother. She held it tight and cried out grievously, and
then was silent. Whatever spell was in the handkerchief had
not done its work. She was on her way to Judgment, and, as
I thought someone should say a word for her, I ran to the
Church next to the Theatre and knelt as close as I could to
the altar.

"Have mercy on mother, Lord God," I begged him. "She

was an old soul free from sin, save that she never married father."

It was whilst I was out and kneeling in unaccustomed prayer that the actors, having come in from their practising, found mother dead. Shakespeare covered her face and it was Sam Crosse who first said the word. "Plague?"

I was told by a number of them when they got to know me, and like me better, what then passed. Shakespeare nodded, and turned to Dick Burbage, who had come in crowned from the rehearsal. "You can take that crown off, Dick," he said, "you're King no longer."

They all knew what he meant. Mother's death must be reported to the Constables. When the audience came they would see no play, only a locked door and a Blue Cross painted, with a notice – "Closed on account of the Plague". Alex Cooke, ever eager in the pursuit of disaster, moved to the door, volunteering to tell the Constable so the Theatre might be closed and the Death Cart take mother.

On his way out fat Will Bell grabbed his arm. "Stop! You want the Death Cart to take our Theatre also?"

"Let him go, Will Bell," Shakespeare said, and then Bell turned on him.

"And you! Are you a poet of such poor ambition you'd let a lump of carrion thwart you?"

"That carrion was a kind old soul, that was of our family," Shakespeare rebuked him, but Bell was determined.

"We tell no one!"

"Keep her here?" Alex Cooke was fearful.

"No. She'll kill us all," said Sam Crosse.

"She must have Christian burial." Shakespeare crossed himself and Burbage clapped him on the shoulder.

"It can't be helped. Tear up your play, Will. I'll sell my crown for a dish of rabbits for the company."

"Tear up my play, as though I never wrote it?"

"We'll meet again next year. When this Plague's over." Burbage tried to sound comforting.

"Next year? Which of us will live to next year? I was to be

heard tomorrow. My play will vanish!" Shakespeare said
bitterly.

"Cheer up, little playmaker. What they don't hear they'll
never miss." Sam Crosse comforted Shakespeare not at all.
He heard the bell tolling from the Church by the plague pit
and then, ever full of invention, bethought him of a plot. He
stood a moment considering and then said quietly, "Church
burial! What the dead don't hear they may not miss either."

"What do you mean, Will?" The actors were looking at him,
puzzled.

"That we might play priests, and perform burial. Quietly."

"You are the Prince of Plotmakers!" Bell was delighted.

"The boy must be told." Shakespeare, it seemed, was the
only one who remembered me. Bell was against it.

"The boy? The boy need know nothing."

"We're all a family, Will Bell. We share all. Remember?"

"You tell him, Will," said Burbage.

So, when I came back from the Church and started to
scrub the stage in case we still might play King Dick on the
morrow, Shakespeare came and put his proposal to me. It
seemed so strange a plan I was quiet a moment, not saying
"yes" or "no" neither, and in that hesitation tasted my new
power, for suddenly everyone wanted to please the scrub-
boy, little Jack Snot Nose.

They gave me a fine supper. Sam Crosse killed the last
capon he had in a cage below the grave trap, and the table
was laid, and I was given a new velvet jacket from the tiring
room and the dagger set with jewels Burbage had worn as the
Duke of York, all because I had not yet agreed to the actors'
plan, or to keep quiet about it. And as I sat on the throne and
ate capon they all thronged round to persuade me. Shakespeare sat nearest, and was the most persuasive.

"She was a good woman, Jack. A good, kind lady. Above all
things she loved this Theatre. Remember how she laboured,
over the hump for my crouchback King." I ate and said
nothing. It was my best course. Shakespeare was almost
pleading. "Well, how would she like, Jack . . .? How could she
*bear* . . . to see all her labour wasted? On the hump, for

instance. She was a part of our play. Just as I or Dick Burbage or you as an attendant page. To see her well-plaited hump wasted. Why, she'd weep for that in Heaven!" I chewed and thought and wondered if a bargain might be struck between us. "They'll shut the Theatre if we tell the Constable, Jack."

"I had no father. Or sisters either." Oh, mother, I thought, what you can do for me now, being dead.

"They'll shut the Theatre for sure, Jack."

"Now I'm alone."

Shakespeare was very comforting. "You have us, Jack. We're your family. And there's a way you can keep your family with you ... Only if you agree."

Now I knew I had them all on the hip. I paused, in acting a pause is most effective, and then I said, "Before I agree to anything. Tell me ..."

"Yes, little Jack. Tell you what?"

Alex Cooke was smiling his sickly grin. So I told them. "Mother will go quietly. But she must have her last wish."

"What wish was that, Jack Rice?" Shakespeare asked me.

"Only that I should play your Lady Anne, King Richard's Queen."

Alex Cooke stopped smiling then, and I knew they couldn't refuse me. In death mother had done as she could not in life, she had made me an actress.

# 13

## Of A Burial At Sea

IT WAS TOM at the Dagger, he who had been poor Kate's husband, that lent the actors his wherry boat.

We trundled all in the cart to the Riverside at night. William Bell shouted out that tomorrow we should give the Tragical History of Richard the Third, with Will Kempe banging his tabor and Alex Cooke looking sick as a miser with a hole in his pocket. And I, little Jack Rice, now Mistress Rice, Chief Actress Rice, Lady Anne and Queen of England Rice, sat on mother's coffin and could not believe my luck.

All went well. It was a dark night and as we came near the river William Bell stopped shouting and the others quieted the drum and music. Then in silence and in shadows the actors carried mother's coffin to the wherry boat (the coffin was that intended for the funeral of my late husband in the play; we had to quickly cobble another together for the next day's performance, but mother got a Royal burial with her box emblazoned with the Arms of the Prince of Wales).

The actors told me that a ship's Captain may lawfully perform a burial, so Dick Burbage was elected Captain of the wherry boat for that night's work, though his knowledge of navigation was somewhat rusty and he was hard put to it to keep our oars from fouling the weeds as we set mother out on her last journey. However, and to give the occasion greater dignity, he wore King Dick's black plume and cloak, and clutched a Bible in his black-gloved hand.

So, with some whispered words appropriate to Burial at Sea, grand as an Admiral in her coffin, mother slipped quietly into the water and by so doing saved our Theatre and the play and made me by her death, as she could not in life, a leading actor. When mother went hugger-mugger into the river began all my fame.

The next day we played King Richard. The groundlings laughed and hissed and shivered at that crafty Monarch's outrageous villainies, the hump that mother plaited perfectly crooked Burbage's back, and I, in my satin and my silken undershirt, in my jewelled stomacher and my fine lawn sleeves, with my rings and my necklets, my full red lips and face white-powdered, my eyes shadowed and sparkling in my new happiness, I, Jack Rice, was surely the most desirable lady ever to be wooed by a King of England.

Now that the Theatres are shut, their galleries pulled down, and acting forbid on pain of a whipping, who is to know, and who can understand how I felt as I trod first on the stage of the Theatre parted as the Lady Anne? I knew all present hushed and looked with pity, not on the scrub-boy who lost a mother, but on the Great and Beautiful Lady who lost a husband and that husband heir to the throne of England.

"Set down, set down your Honourable load," I commanded the bearers. I had practised, during many a quiet evening scrubbing, how to speak so the words fell gently but clearly into the circle of that Theatre like pebbles into water, so that none was missed and yet none was trumpeted. And the groundlings kept so still, and listened so attentively to a lady in distress that I felt I could keep them for ever listening, only releasing them when I had a mind to, and that I could bring their tears but with a break in a line, or a glance of my big, sad, painted eyes towards them. How proud I was, how brave in my unprotected grief and female loneliness when the toad Richard the Third Burbage came to woo my delicate person.

I must remember, I needs must remember, for I have all the lines and cues in my head as though it were yesterday,

how proudly I told Burbage of the virtues of that coffined
body.

"His better does not breathe upon the earth."

"He lives that loves thee better than he could."

Then I gave them a trumpet call of defiance, high and true,
something to stir the blood of the groundlings.

"Name him!"

"Plantagenet." I liked the way Burbage said it, like a
low roll of drums.

"Why, what was he?"

"The self-same name but of a better nature."

"Where is he?"

"Here!" Burbage's face was grinning, ingratiating, lecherous and quite contemptible. Now came my moment. In
honour of all the days spent scrubbing the stage, being yelled
at as Jack Bare Arse and sent to empty piss-pots or run
errands, I filled my cheeks with spit and fired it at Burbage
and found the target dead between his eyes. Oh how I blessed
Will Shakespeare for giving that direction ("She spits at
him"!)

And when I spat that great globule of revenge how they
all cheered, and were cheering still when Crookback Richard
died at Bosworth (where Alex Cooke was parted as "one
dead") and after all was done they stood ten minutes cheering.

"We are made men!" Sam Crosse shouted as we came into
the tiring room. Will Kempe cut a caper and Bell promised us
strong ale and beefs daily and Hemminge and Condell
counted the cash and said that at the next playing would all
our expenditure be paid. I was before the mirror staring at
my beauty (I could not see enough of it then and now I flinch
from my reflection and avoid a looking glass) when Burbage
thought to patronise my playing with a little moderate praise.

"You did not badly, little Jack Rice. You shall do better
when you learn not to gabble and to hold your pauses."

"And you shall do better, Burbage," I said, "when you do
not stand betwixt me and the audience in the coffin scene.
Do you remember, they pay to see me also."

"Has no one a boot for that boy's buttocks!" Will Bell

muttered, I now think most understandably, although the others hushed him, I having their necks all in my control. As I turned on Bell he changed his tune and muttered politely, "Why, Jack, now you are an actor truly. Your mother would have been proud to see it."

"She would have grieved to hear you miss your cue as Lord Mayor, Bell. It's the ale, I take it. It starts to rot your brain." Who can remember their early triumphs without shame? Truly I have more to blush for than most. I saw Bell's itching toe almost fly from the ground, but Burbage, sighing, disappointed him.

"Careful, Bell," he said. "We must all care for little Jack Rice now."

And as though to emphasise his point there came a great rapping at the door and trembling Alex Cooke opened to two large Constables of the Watch.

"We have reports of one sick here or hereabouts," said the largest, reddest Constable. "Have you knowledge of a Mistress Rice?"

There was a silence then in the tiring room as full of fear and foreboding as we had heard in the Theatre when Burbage saw the ghosts before the Field of Bosworth. Truly, our actors must have thought this was the way of life for a player, one moment capering triumphant in the tiring room, with his ears full of applause and his head full of the pile of coin to come in the week's performances, and the next facing nothing but the Theatre barred and silent and his own death or imprisonment for hiding the Plague and performing a Burial most Blasphemous.

"I know Mistress Rice. I am her only child." I stepped forward, my lips still scarlet and my face powdered so that the Constable looked puzzled whether to condole with one bereaved or pinch the buttock of something, boy or girl, that stirred his sluggish lechery.

"Look you, Officers. This boy's mother . . ." Shakespeare had been silent since we took our bows. There was a sadness about him, as if the giving of the play had seemed but a small conclusion to the great task of disposing of the dead. His speech was broken and he began again, "Officers. He needs must tell you ..."

The others looked at him, dumbstruck and filled with horror. I knew he had revolted at the Un-Christian Act of Burial; but his way of atonement was far too dangerous, and it would have cut short my precious life as an actor. I moved to the Constable, fluttered my lashes (mother had been careful to pare them when I was a baby, so they grew thick and languorous) gave him a whiff of my Royal perfumes and spoke to him as if we were alone and I had all to promise.

"Mother's gone into the country, Constable," I smiled and laid a white hand on his doublet. "You see, she fears the plague."

Why should he not believe me? The Officers thanked me and left. And so I saved the company.

\* \* \*

"You want my protection?" Hal sat with his feet in an ewer of Rose Water, relishing the story of mother's burial, which had driven his poet back to him.

"You know the Magistrates and Judges. You may even know the Councillors."

"Oh, I do, Will, and I know their wives also."

"We had two Constables calling, which the cunning child did contrive to satisfy. But if there be more enquirings ..."

"You would have a Patron, is that it, Will? As your Protector?"

"At least a friend about the Court. Are there not ways the matter might be settled?"

"Oh, there are ways, Will." Hal's feet were dried now by Hercules and he stood up, almost angry. "By God, this plague does more than kill. 1 think so. Such things are men driven to – out of the fear of it." And then he smiled. "You conniving, cunning plot-sharpener! You flame of ambition!"

"You do well to mock!"

"Your family! That little family of the Theatre you are so loyal to. And one dies!" Hal was laughing now, delighted

"So you drop her in the river lest she should hinder a poet's ambition."

"I have regretted it. Bitterly."

"Regret nothing!" Now Hal's hand was on his shoulder. "You were blinded by this Theatre. It was your little world, so dark and narrow! Nothing else mattered. Not life. Nor death. Not love even."

"Not love?"

"I told you! There's a world outside, a world full of air and light and sunshine. Inhabited by Lords and cut-purses and those who never learned a line or practised a death fall, or buried an old lady for the sake of a performance."

"Your world, my Lord Privilege?" Shakespeare, it seemed, was still resisting it.

"Our world, Will. Where I have invited you."

Shakespeare, it seems, was considering the invitation, when they heard a great beating at the door below. Hal sent young Hercules down to tell whoever knocked that his Lordship was dead of the plague and could see no one. He looked at Shakespeare with the excitement of one who holds the high cards at Primero, and feels in his tingling thumbs that the next game is one he's bound to win. And no doubt Shakespeare already sniffed the sunshine through beech trees, and the primrose walks of that country far from the stench of plague and the fever of plotting in the Theatre.

But below Hercules had let in none other than one of our players, Augustine Phillips, who, hearing that Will Shakespeare had gone to Southampton House to seek out a protector, ran after him with fresh news of our troubles.

"You may not come in!" The boy page Hercules was trying to bar Augustine's way. "My Lord Southampton is dead."

"I care not for your Lord Southampton." Phillips pushed his way in most unmannerly. "I have news for our playmaker. Is he upstairs?" For from the shadows up the marble stair-case Phillips heard voices.

"His Lordship left strict instructions. He's not to be disturbed when he's dead!" Hercules had hold of Phillips' doublet like a terrier; but the actor shook him off strongly,

bounded up the staircase and pushed open the door behind
which he thought he had heard a Poet and his Patron. And
there he was greeted by a sight most solemn and funereal.

Hal was stretched out on the bed, his eyes closed, his hands
joined in prayer, just as if he were lying in marmoreal im-
mobility on the top of his tomb at Titchfield. And Shakespeare, kneeling in that same attitude of respectful mourning
which the graven child Hal will adopt for all eternity at his
Father's tomb, spoke a prayer extempore.

"*Henricus Southamptoniensis, in vino veritas, in flagrante
delictu, pro bona publico. Amen.*" Not dog but bitch Latin
you might have called it.

"Will!" Shakespeare turned and saw Augustine Phillips,
his hat snatched off kneeling respectfully beside him. Only
a matter of the utmost urgency could have caused him to
invade a Lord's Death Chamber. "Will Bell is taken sorely
sick." The words poured out of Phillips. "And Dick Burbage
says we cannot drop *him* in the river or surely he'd float to
Greenwich. So the Constables are informed. The Theatre is
closed. The cart is packed. And we are to go into the country
to play in all the Town Halls and Inns, for Dick says whatever
we do we must keep the family together. Will you come,
Will?"

"Or will you stay with me?" Lord Lazarus of Southampton
opened his eyes and sat up, sending Augustine Phillips leaping to the doorway as though his toes were singed with Hell
fire all of a sudden. It seemed that Shakespeare hesitated,
but then he answered, even if something reluctantly, the call
of his family in trouble and went with Augustine Phillips. He
left Hal smiling, for though he had not got his own way
entirely, at least he had near frightened an actor to death.

# 14

## Of A Family Parting

SO OUR ACTORS' cart was loaded once again. It was cold, damp and foggy, a November morning to bite your fingers and stifle your throat and we were all (except for mother and William Bell, gone on a different journey) stamping our feet and blowing our fingernails when Will Shakespeare came up to us carrying his bundle. He slung it onto the cart among the thrones, coffins and costumes and then pulled himself up beside me. He was in a silent sort that morning and would not return my greeting, so I knew not if he were brooding on a new play or cursing his company.

"We shall visit your home, Will," Dick Burbage shouted. "We shall play at Stratford!"

At this news Shakespeare seemed but to sink into a deeper gloom, and a silence more profound.

"Shall we set forth then, Hearts, to New Conquests and Glories yet undreamed of?" One of Burbage's chief defects was his insane cheerfulness in the early morning, brought about, no doubt, by the huge mess of beef, bread and coddled eggs, washed down by the thin wine he took for breakfast. I knew all these Glories from my infancy, draughty inns, stables to sleep in, and an audience of yokels who tried to kiss those parted as girls, pelted the villains with farm ordure and ran screaming from the ghosts.

So the cart started to trundle and we passed the Theatre, our Theatre, locked and barred now, with the Blue Cross

painted on it and the Notice fixed by the direction of the
Privy Council closing it as a place wherein infection may be
increased and to which recourse was therefore forbid.

So as we rattled out of the town leaving behind us our
Theatre (and also much fear of death), I, in my new-found
glory, rallied the silent Shakespeare.

"You are dreaming of a new part for me, Uncle Will?"

"For *you*?" I remember his head rose slowly from his hands
and he looked on me as though I were some strange being
from another world into which he had strayed and took no
pleasure in.

"Oh, I am to have all the great girl-roles now. Dick Burbage
can refuse me nothing!"

"Can he not?"

I rattled on, foolish as a wife who never guesses she is
saying the very words that must drive her husband from her.
"I would fancy a comedy, Uncle Will. I love to hear them
laugh. And I was thinking. Not to give me the perpetual
weight of a petticoat, might not our heroine disguise herself
in breeches? To counterfeit a boy!"

"You have been looking at my papers." It was true. I had.

"Shall you have my comedy finished Will, by the time we
come to Stratford? Or must I lock you up – as did old Ned
Alleyn?"

"*Your* comedy? My plays are *yours* now." He was very
quiet, and I was very sure.

"You write for me. Remember, Uncle Will, I have no family
but you, since I lost mother."

I spoke of mother but to remind him of the tale I might
tell, were there not a comedy with a good girl part in it, or
should there be any dangerous talking of putting the doleful
Alex Cooke back into my petticoats.

Now I know not what precisely his good wife Anne said
which made Will Shakespeare shoulder his bundle and walk
silently out of doors and stay away that long time without a
word of remembrance. What word is it that so quick can
snap the chain that binds a family? I am sure now that she
reminded him of his duty, or his obligations, or the gratitude

he owed her, or the terrible consequences of his neglecting his part as a father by not chopping kindling wood or not rebuking the children. And I reminded him of his duty to see me properly provided with a part in return for my Great Sacrifice in respect of Mother's Death. "You took me from my father and five others that might have married me, one being a lawyer!" "I saw mother sink unhallowed and is this your gratitude?" "Chop the firewood!" "Write the comedy!" "Is this what husbands, this what playmakers are for?" I had played a wife, had grown shrill and demanding also. He looked at me, much as he might have looked at her, as though I were not there, and called on Alex Cooke to pass his bundle.

When he had it he jumped off the tail of the cart as we were passing through Holborn. He walked quickly away and would not look back at us, the actors, although we called, shouted and pleaded with him. Our family ties were broken and it was a year before I saw him again.

Hal was standing in a fur gown by the crackling perfumed logs in the great room at Southampton House. He looked up at his visitor as if he had long been expecting him, as if he were only a little late.

"So you are come back. What must I protect you from now?"

"Bad dreams."

So Shakespeare slept again in silken sheets and woke again to the cry of peacocks. And the next day he and Hal rode down to Titchfield, across the downs and through the iced woods, where they would hunt the deer and fish for trouts, and my Uncle Will's only task was to write such verses as should set Hal the Horse-thief apart from the rest of us who must die and be quite forgotten.

# Part Three

## "OF COMFORT AND DESPAIR"

*"Two loves I have of comfort and
    despair
Which like two spirits do suggest me
    still;
The better angel is a man right fair,
The worser spirit a woman coloured
    ill."*

Sonnet 144

# 15

## Of What Was Revealed
## By The Death Of Tybalt

I WAS GIVING my Lady Juliet, one of my favourite roles and
for which I shall long be remembered. (I saw old Master
Pennybroker, our Rector's father, look quaintly at me in
Church last Sunday as if trying to recollect something. Did
he see me down a misty corridor of memory as a Star Crossed
Lover, married at fourteen, hauling her husband up a balcony
to spreadeagle her upon an Italian mattress on a hot night in
Verona? Did his thought grow so hot in memory that he
would have crossed the aisle to pinch my aged buttock? As
we passed in the graveyard I thought I heard him whisper,
"A rose by any other name would smell as sweet." It was like
a password given by allies lost in battle, and, though I have
not changed this old shirt for a fortnight, I was grateful
for it.)

When I gave my Lady Juliet (they were turning men away
from the Theatre and the Lords paid more than a crown to
sit upon the stage and hear me, and greatly more than that
to take me to supper afterward) I swear that Will Shakespeare, who played my cousin Tybalt, had his eyes less on
me or the other actors than searching the groundlings, quest-
ing, endlessly for a face. There is a scene in that old play
(forgotten now and never again to be acted) at a great dance
and gathering at the Capulet's to which Romeo appears
masked. Now when Burbage as Romeo was courting me,
Tybalt was meant to be protesting to my father at the vile

manners of Romeo, a Montague, intruding on our revels. But Will Shakespeare instead of looking at my father, or seeming in the least concerned with the family quarrels was scanning the audience, row by row. At first I thought he was Counting Heads, so he could better calculate his share of shillings. But, as he came to an end and grew towards his exit line, I saw his face light up in most contented recognition. It went thus:

### TYBALT
"Patience perforce with wilful choler meeting
  Makes my flesh tremble at their different greeting
  I will withdraw . . ."

(As he says this Tybalt's eye lights upon a young but well-formed, dark-haired, big-eyed youth among the groundlings, who is wearing a leather jerkin and an orange velvet cap pulled down low over his eyes. Tybalt thereupon greets this youth with a grin; a furtive lifting of his hand from the hilt of his sword on which he has relaxed his grip a little, and a small and most inappropriate bow.)

"... but this intrusion shall
  Now seeming sweet, convert to bitter gall!"

(Exit Tybalt in the best of possible humours, smiling broadly.)

Now it so happened that I was not the only one watching Shakespeare and the one he was watching. Hal, Earl of Southampton, was that day among the groundlings also, preferring that position to the eminence of the stage where he had to listen to gossip concerning yesterday's jousts or which of Her Majesty's Ladies had most recent cause to let out her stomacher; besides which Hal had an idea to surprise Will by coming to the play which he had heretofore avoided as an idle tale of love, and what was even more tedious, not of love for the Earl of Southampton, either. So Hal was there in his horse-thief's doublet and frayed old cap, for when the play was done he thought of how he and Will might run through Cheapside and Holborn, consorting with Foists and Robbers, bowsing on bastard ale, and sharing all from pigeon stewed to pot-girls. So Hal noticed Tybalt's wandering eye, and the notable concern of his friend the actor for a certain scrubbed boy among the groundlings.

After the scene at the ball Dick Burbage wooed me in the orchard: telling me that the fairest stars in heaven used my eyes to twinkle for them when they were away on business. Whatever business do stars have? I wonder. The sale of Furs and Sweet Wines in the City, or do they lie about their whereabouts and are they secretly off bedding pot-girls or tumbling curling boys? These lines, like many Will Shakespeare wrote in this love story, should not be enquired into too deeply. Suffice it to say that the way Dick Burbage Romeoed me on the stage brought me near to tears, so convinced was I of my own delectable beauty, although Burbage never even ruffled my hair or kissed my cheek in the tiring room, which is more than can be said of that long streak of canting lechery, Alex Cooke. Then came my marriage in the cell of that old idiot and worst of plotmakers Friar Lawrence, and after it a fight in the streets where Cousin Tybalt slays Romeo's friend Mercutio and shortly thereafter, by a quick jab of Romeo's rapier, is sent to join the Jesting Mercutio in the sky.

It was this scene, the death of Tybalt, that set Hal Southampton on a trail which well nigh led to the death of a friendship. I saw what he saw and wondered greatly at it, but I did not follow Hal in his quest after the truth of the matter and only heard the whole tale many years after, when Will Shakespeare and I were drunk as two Lords one Christmas night in Holborn, and we were talking of the maze of lies and double-dealing which all men must enter without a single thread to guide them, should they be mad enough to fall in love.

It will be seen from what I have said touching the fights in *Romeo and Juliet* that this was a play full of blood. In fact Sam Crosse used to go down each morning to the slaughter house to fill those pig's bladders the actors wore slung beneath their armpits. When the tip of the rapier pricked the

bladder, why then a great quantity of blood would spurt out
of him wounded in a manner most alarming and natural (I
have heard a simple-minded groundling swear we killed a
couple of actors at each performance, which I should not
have minded had we had that long nasal fool Alex Cooke
parted as Tybalt).

Now I from behind the curtain of the Inner Stage, and
Hal from the ground, were both watching the boy in the
orange velvet cap as Romeo engaged Tybalt. And as Tybalt-
Shakespeare fought, he was regarding Romeo far less than
Master Velvet Cap. In due course Romeo's rapier flashed
through Tybalt's defences, which were not well played that
afternoon, no doubt because of his concern with the boy in
the audience. And then we, that is Hal and I, saw the pig's
bladder beneath Shakespeare's shirt nicked by the rapier,
and squeezed by the actor to give greater encouragement to
a fountain of blood which gushed crimson into the air, falling
onto the stage in a great pool which looked more like the
stainings of Agincourt than a small family feud in an Italian
Square.

At the sight of which young Master Velvet Cap went pale
as Shakespeare's shirt before the fighting, and he fainted dead
away.

Well, the play was so popular that it was hard to put a
paper between the groundlings, so that the boy had no chance
of falling, being propped up, as you can tell, by the bodies
around him, and in a few seconds he was recovered, and
indeed was standing again with colour back in his cheeks by
the time the Duke entered to pronounce Romeo banished.
But this sight of the fainting groundling (groundlings
being well used to blood at bear-baits and hangings) no doubt
interested Hal extremely. When the play ended (with me dead
in my tomb and all the Theatre weeping for the pity of it) he
fought his way out among the press, although we ever saw
that orange cap float away among the crowds in front of him.

Outside the Theatre, however, Hal saw the fastidious boy
met by a most imposing and dignified creature, a tall speci-
men in black clothes, with a gold chain about his neck, the

appearance of a nasty smell beneath his nose, bearing in his
right hand a tall stick mounted with a silver knob, and in
his left a silken cord at the end of which danced and yapped
a little lap-dog. Beside this edifice of pomposity the boy
walked quickly, his head well down and his eyes studying the
pavement as though he could read his fortune in it. Hal the
Horse-thief came up to them, took off his battered bonnet,
bowed low and started what he hoped was a friendly conversation.

"You fainted, young sir, when Tybalt was run through."
At which the lap-dog yapped, the tall man with the Nasty
Smell under his Nose waved his long wand and said, "Give
way, there fellow. Give way!" in a voice such as the Archbishop of Canterbury might use if he found a pile of dog-shit
before the High Altar. "This young gentleman is of good
family. Nobly born. He speaks neither to players, nor those
who frequent playhouses." With that he moved on, and the
boy said nothing.

"It was but counterfeit." Hal walked after the boy. "They
use blood from a pig's bladder. Near enough a pint of red
blood tucked under the arm to gush forth at a stabbing." At
which news, far from being reassured, the young gentleman
went green again, a change of colour which led Hal to ask,
"Are you not squeamish for a gentleman?"

"Go your ways, uncouth fellow. Prattle of pig's bladders
to those of your own station. My young master will go home
to rest."

The end of the staff swinging jabbed Hal in the knees. He
stopped and called after the retreating couple, "On a scented
day-bed? Fanned by peacock's feathers?"

Hal was not to be shaken off by the tallest lackey, waving
the longest staff, and he was interested by that one sentence
–"Speaks not to players." So he followed down several
narrow streets, past rows of ill-favoured dwellings, until the
Master and his Servant came to a small apothecary's shop,
with an old stuffed crocodile hung out as a sign over the
low doorway. It was into this dusty place, with its pots of
herbs and Jars of specifics for various diseases just visible

behind the dirty windows, that the strange couple went.

Hal went into the tavern opposite and ordered a pint of bastard ale. He sat in the tavern window from which he had a fine view of the apothecary's. He had hardly taken a gulp before the tall servant came out alone, leaving the boy inside.

As Hal finished the mug he saw Shakespeare come quickly along the street and go into the shop. He was smiling.

Five slow mugs of bastard later, and almost an hour gone by the clock, the servant returned and went into the shop. This time he was without the lap-dog. Hal ordered another pint mug.

After two good gulps the servant came out with – Hal spluttered his ale and blew forth all over the pot-girl as he saw it – with a young woman, fairly dressed, with dark hair, a cheek of rose velvet, and the self-same height and features as the Boy who Fainted at the Sight of Blood.

What was this apothecary's? A shop for turning Men into Maids but at the swallowing of a herbal draught and the eating of stewed Mandrake?

Hal watched as the Lady and her servant went off down the street.

His waiting was rewarded. By the time he had finished this mug he saw Shakespeare come out and leave in another direction; he was not smiling nor did he look like a man who had enjoyed his afternoon.

Hal sat still after this friend had gone, and did not make himself known to him. I believe he was still smiling, but in his heart he was cold and angry that his friend should keep secrets from him, and not be faithful.

# 16

## *Of How Shakespeare Escaped One Plague And Contracted Another*

I TOLD YOU of Shakespeare when he jumped off our cart at the time of the Great Sickness. And now we have him sliding furtively into an apothecary's shop where, it seems, in place of changing base metal into gold, they turned sensitive boys into intriguing ladies but at the drop of a pair of small hose and the twitch of a petticoat. So I must tell you what befell Will Shakespeare and his patron in the time between his riding down to Titchfield and his return to us.

When they rode through the mists and winter woods Hal and Will Shakespeare were laughing all the way, and they laughed a great deal from then till after Christmas, whether out hunting deer, coursing at the hare with swift greyhounds, shooting at small fowl, pheasant and grype with the stone bow or the Caliver, or hawking at the partridge with soar hawks and haggards and other species of Falcon. Other diversions were playing bouts with Hal's wrestler Frederick, who always contrived to throw his master into the dung heap, and riding on Hal's mounts, those fine Spanish, Neapolitan and Barbary steeds, which he could command with a whisper, or a flick of his smallest finger on the reigns, and who would dance a Galliard or a Courante for him, or fly over the highest leap as if winged, for whatever his other faults might be Hal was certainly the finest, most delicate horseman in England, which is surely why he adopted the title of "Hal the Horse-thief" when he took to Roguery

And then, in January, Hal began to ask Will Shakespeare on their morning rides, or to shout at him from under the huge bulk of Frederick the wrestler who seemed always happily engaged in breaking his Lordship's arm for him, if he had written good verses the night before.

"Oh, yes," Shakespeare said once to such a question. "As your house-cow gives thick cream and your pullets lay fresh eggs, so your house-poet has laid twenty-five stanzas before breakfast." Hal laughed and put his Rome Barbary to a high stone wall, not choosing to hear, in Will's reply, the first note of rebellion.

In February one of the Spanish mares was delivered of a foal. It was a night of high excitement with two farm servants, Hal and his Moorish groom working with their sleeves rolled up in the sweet smelling, blood-stained straw of the stable, and Will Shakespeare sitting on a block looking on, and little Hercules pouring white wine for his master and Bastard Ale for his master's servants (although Shakespeare got wine, as a kind of privileged or superior retainer). When the foal was safely born Hal sat with his hand on its sticky little head and said wearily, "Must I have an heir?"

"Sure, with such fine stock to breed from," Shakespeare told him.

"So! To be remembered, to continue, to be something other than dust. I must labour in bed. I must marry old Burghley's grand-daughter, I must provide doweries and marriage settlements for brats I hope may produce male brats also, to keep my name tottering through time; work you can do in half an hour before breakfast with a broken pen and a set of rhymes borrowed out of the Italian."

"If it rouses you so. You write the verses. I'll marry a Countess."

"I could get no rhymes. And you no high born lady."

"True. But I have more chance to stray into a coroneted bed sheet than you into couplets."

"And your couplets, of course, will make you deathless!" Hal was looking at Shakespeare with a sort of envy. And Shakespeare could not find it in him to deny the suggestion.

"We each must build – our own monument. Mine is safer than an heir. Verses are free from the Spanish sickness," he said.

And then Hal laughed. "When I marry, *if* I marry, will we still hunt game birds at Titchfield, you and I?"

"If your wife allows you so much liberty."

Hal flinched at the thought of such matrimonial bondage, and went back to seek comfort near the steaming foal. "Must I start *now*. To populate a Nursery?" His voice was plaintive. "Am I grown so old?"

Then Shakespeare quoted some pieces of flattery he had written.

"To me, fair friend, you never can be old. Don't you *read* the verses I make for you?"

In March the Spring came and the fresh winds blew the plague from London. We actors came back to the Theatre. We had gone a long way and made a little money, but we were grown weary of sleepy towns and groundlings who stared in wonder if an actor who had been killed got up to make his bow ("A ghost! A ghost!" they cried in Bury St. Edmunds, and all rushed screaming out of the inn yard we played in). To be back in London seemed to us to be born again. To find girls who smelt not of dung and to play to an audience who knew that Rome was not a village in the next county, or Athens a kind of rare fruit, was a delight after a long deprivation. We came back to all we had before, save that we had no playmaker.

In April when the daffodils were out in the woods at Titchfield, Shakespeare, who had admired the schooling of a Spanish horse, said to Hal, "How would it please you to give up all your horses and hunting and occupations here?" To which Hal answered that he would feel half dead. "Then you can understand how I feel being parted from the Theatre."

"But I would forsake all this and twenty more estates for the sake of our friendship," said Hal, and rode away, hoping he had settled the matter.

\*　　\*　　\*

What manner of friendship was it then, between this poet and that Lord? It is a question that must be enquired into, although only at night, and behind the locked door of this vestry; but I can tell you only what I know of it, and what I have heard, and the final answer must be yours to decide on as you will.

First may be asked what drew them together, when their stations in life were so different. There was a learned Doctor here, caught in a hay loft with his serving wench, a girl but thirteen with no letters in her head, who yet denied adultery. Asked what drove him to this chit's company he answered, "Why, only that we discussed the wisdom of Seneca together." He was not believed. But it can well be thought that Poet and Peer had much to talk of, besides their common experiences of the world of thieves. And it's certain Hal thought himself in need of a verse-maker who could cheat death for him, and Shakespeare found in the company of such lively beauty of form and person that which made him careless of whether his verses made either one of them immortal or no.

During this time Hal was often summoned to appear at Court and coming back reported all that had been said by the Queen and the Great Lords and those sweet Ladies, tumbled as often as nine-pins in the Royal Gardens, who were called the Queen's "Glories". All this was necessary information to Will, who would make Kings and Queens and Great Lords in the Theatre, and where could he better learn their tongue than at the Earl of Southampton's table? When I think of the plays, I remember he could write Panders and Princes, Rogues and Royalty well; but there are few solid burghers or honest shop-keepers there. So his characters seem to come either from the Jolly Struggler or Titchfield Abbey. So may his long friendship with Hal be explained other than by lusts and passion.

When at Titchfield, Shakespeare also had occasion to meet Hal's mother, who had become a garrulous old dame and, perhaps because of her light behaviours in the past, found it no shame to prattle to a Poet and a Playmaker (unlike some of the well-born guests who sat above the salt and would not think it at all befitting to talk to one who came from the brothel world of the London Theatres. Such a proud Popinjay was Southampton's exquisite cousin Anthony Browne, who thought it an insult that any servant should turn his back upon his master's roast while it was a'cooking. Him Will Shakespeare frightened so by dressing as an old woman whom the first Earl had burned at the stake come back to haunt Titchfield, that Master Browne ran screeching out of the Abbey one Twelfth Night and was never seen there more.) As I say the old Countess spoke much to Shakespeare of her longing to see her Hal with an heir, and he repeated her advice, somewhat improved as to the expression, in the verses he wrote her son: but I question whether he was mightily concerned as to his friend's feats of fatherhood, I think he rather wrote these lines to calm an old lady whose past had been too exciting and whose present too dull.

It is true that in one of the poems he wrote to Hal, Shakespeare spoke of that addition which doting nature bestowed upon his patron (whom he there called his "Master-Mistress") whereby he was defeated of the enjoyment of his beloved who, he agrees, was "prickt" out for women's pleasure. Some may think this verse closes the door on all speculation; but I, who know all the stir and scandal caused when these same sonnets first became public, think this may be a verse added to silence those who might suspect that Hal, though "prickt", was not thereby placed beyond the full reach of him whose passion is therein made clear. On the other side I must agree that Shakespeare, unlike his teacher Marlowe, would rather lie with a girl or a woman if one could be had, and although he may have been bewitched by some boys, he never, by a nod, a wink, or a hand to the waist, far less to the buttock, made me a suggestion when I was young and parted as all his Fairest Ladies. This I find most strange.

And what of Hal? He at that time set his face most stubborn against breeding, and was so firm against obeying his guardian's command to marry with Lady Vere, that old

Burghley, as he was empowered to do by law, fined him
£5,000 all to be paid at once. This Hal did, although it left
his estate sorely maimed, and Lady Vere earned fame through
England as the woman it cost most not to tumble. I believe
Hal thought all women then as false as his mother, and, in
his heart, Shakespeare had no rival.

So I sit here, a chilly old man writing in a blanket and
mittens, who has less chance of sporting between silken
sheets with a young Earl than of becoming Lord Chief Justice
of England. And it seems to me I must be done with this
key-hole spying and there shall be no more of it. If they did
not the act of darkness, which is the act of loving, they could
not have loved each other more; and if they did it they could
not thereby have loved each other less.

I hold to the opinion, all things being considered, that they
did. Let us say no more upon the subject but proceed with
our history.

* * *

So things went until the Summer when there came a knocking
at the great doors of Titchfield and on them being opened at
the Lord's command in came a little boy walking on his
hands, to be followed by one turning cartwheels, to be followed by a whole cry of players and a waggon load of crowns
and costumes and Hal, thinking to divert Shakespeare who
had fallen, since the warm weather, into a kind of melancholy,
a very slough of silence, invited them to play after dinner.
This they did, giving an old comedy, and afterward danced
a burgomask. It was but shoddily done and Will smiled little
on it – but when it was over and the actors sent down to take
beef and small beers with the servants he stayed silent and
would not even give his opinion of the actors.

That night Hal came to him in his bedchamber and said,
"Have your way, Will, go back to your Theatre. Only lodge
with me at Southampton House."

I think Hal also gave him money to contribute to our

players : which seeing that he was ever jealous of the Theatre, thinking of it as a rival, was an act of love *non pareil*.

\* \* \*

So Shakespeare came back to us and to a most hearty welcome. He wrote us several Comedies, one about that company of strolling players that came one night to Titchfield, and two plays historical, one being the account of the Great Deposition of the Second Richard, which was to bring him to such dangers in the years to come. I was something nervous of his return, seeing it was one look at little Jack Rice as a nagging wife which had caused him to take his bundle from the cart and leave our company in the first place. But when he was back he seemed to bear me no ill-will but parted me as his Shrew (no doubt in tribute to my nagging) and when I gave that vile hussy life, he seemed pleased with me and I continued as his leading girl-actor and was such at the time I told you of, when I was Juliet and he a distracted Tybalt, looking for a boy among the groundlings.

There was a difference, all the same, in Will Shakespeare when he returned from Titchfield. He was smiling often, courteous also, but it was not only his new dress, his suit of black satin and lace cuffs that stood him apart from us. He lodged then at Southampton House, and none of *us* went home after the play to perfumed logs and bowls of rose water and nightly dinners of partridge and pheasant, not even Dick Burbage, although by the size of his belt you could tell our Theatre prospered. But it was as if Shakespeare had been let into a secret world which we should never see, and been made part of its mysteries. I remember even I thought he had moved into a sphere above us mortals, until I found him in love and sunk as deep in the mud as any of us.

One night we actors were called to play in the Hall of the Middle Temple, Palace of Lawyers. We had by then played at Court and were known as the Lord Chamberlain's Men, and Shakespeare had a share of this company from the money his Earl had given him, as had Burbage and the leading

actors, so we thought it no great thing to be called to play
before lawyers, many of whom, their bellies being full of
good red Burgundy wines, slept and snuffled throughout our
comedy (the play was an old one, *Two Gentlemen of Verona*).
But the Learned Masters of the Bench of that Society brought
with them their Ladies, who might safely spy actors, being
in the Company of Hanging Judges and lying Lawyers and
not among poor honest groundlings who never sent one to
the rope nor spun a crafty story. And one Master of the
Bench in particular, that hanger *non pareil*, old Justice
Fleminge, brought with him his young wife Mary, a girl
with the most wonderfully lust-promising eye, the most dan-
gerously curved lip, the darkest hair and the sweetest,
creamiest bubbies to be seen this side of Temple Bar.

She was the daughter of a City Tailor to whom the Judge
repaired for a new pair of breeches to cover his old rump
while he sat on the Bench a'hanging. Mary was about the
shop, with her mouth full of pins helping to stitch and sew,
when the Judge's eye fell upon her, and having his old lust
stirred by certain whore's whippings he had that day ordered,
he made sure to win and woo her. (The first Mrs. Justice
Fleminge had died, some said of a plague, but I say of the
tedium of listening to her husband's tales of Merry Quips
made on Hanging Days on the North-Eastern Circuit.) Now
you may think it a hard task for an old man whose machinery
will scarce stir for less than a sentence of the lash (and only as
much for that as his scarlet robe might well conceal) to woo
and win such a young girl as Mary. But a little gold goes a
long way with a tailor, and the prospect of marriage to One
of Her Majesty's Judges seemed no mean ambition to Mary
or her family. So, at this playing of *Two Gentlemen of Verona*
at the Inner Temple, Mary Fleminge sat in the state of a
velvet-covered chair beside her husband, who slept (a task
which he performed with great skill on the Bench, after
dinner or in bed) and only snored *sotto voce*. And Mary
Fleminge, who was a great sigher over poems and ballads,
a great laugher at Comedies and weeper at Tragic Odes and
Sad Madrigals, watched the piece with her eyes shining, in

love with all the play and the players, including me, Jack Rice, tricked out in the breeches of a well-reputed page which was the Lady Julia in disguise. I know not if she thought me a boy or a girl but as either I was beautiful.

After the play with the true Grace of Lawyers we were received by the Masters of the Bench and their Ladies, before being taken to the Buttery to feast on such ales as the servants had watered down and such hens as proved too tough for the students.

"Master Shakespeare" – the Learned Justice Fleminge was awake now and felt all the glow of morning – "my good wife found your piece vastly entertaining. I am not often at the playhouse. We have so little time now, with so many villains and rascals to be hung up."

"And you, madam. Do you go to the playhouse?" Shakespeare told me his voice then sounded to him like the voice of a stranger, issuing from a long way off. He felt as one who had been taken with the Great Sickness, that is to say his palms itched, his knees turned to water, his head was either so cold that it seemed on fire or so hot that it felt freezing, his privates stung and throbbed as though he had fallen among stinging nettles, but, and such was the power of this malady, it was a disease which he felt only a longing to increase and never be cured. And all this happened, so quick can such disaster befall, but as he bowed before the dark and promising eyes, the small contemptuous nose and high white bubbies of Mrs. Fleminge, wife to the Justice.

"Oh, no, Master Shakespeare. I am forbid to go."

"I cannot have my wife seen in playhouses," Mr. Justice Fleminge explained. "One of the Queen's Justices cannot have his wife seen in such places." With that he passed on to condescend to Burbage.

"Still, you might go there disguised." Shakespeare was left for only a few seconds alone with the Judge's wife.

"Disguised? How should I disguise?"

"Why, put on breeches. Like Lady Julia in my play."

I think it was that thought of going out into a strange world in breeches that most excited her.

# 17

## *Of Breeches Parts, Petticoat Parts And The Sin Of Self-Love*

ON THE DAY my mother, God rest her soul, her bones must now be drifted near to France, or up to the coast of Norseland, on the day my poor mother by dying got me the part of the Lady Anne, I first tore down my breeches and felt against my thighs and cool upon my codpiece the sweet rustle of silk. I sat, as I recall it, my bum bare against the petticoats and widened my eyes with a shading of burnt cork, freshened my cheeks with a red rouge, turned my lips to deep coral and powder whitened my neck to a pillar of alabaster. And when I looked at myself in the tiring-room mirror, for sure I found myself irresistible. That seed which had no chance to germinate when I was but a scrubby boy with a snot nose and black fingernails grew to a full flower; I was overcome by the sin of self-love.

So I think was it with Mistress Mary Fleminge when, but to visit privily a public playhouse and keep the Judge from hearing of her escapades, she climbed into tight-fitting hose and saw most of her fine leg, clamped her sweet box of delights into a boy's breeches, buttoned her bubbies tight in a man's shirt and tucked her long black hair into a cap of red velvet. She glanced, I do believe, into a fine gilt mirror in her bedchamber, fell head-over-heels in love with the young gallant she saw there and really needed no other lover Which was a sorry state of affairs for Will Shakespeare.

Not that he knew or even suspected that her love was more

to herself than any lover, be he the most elegant Poet or the greatest Playmaker. He was most powerfully led by the nose; for her behaviours, light indeed for the wife of a scarlet Judge, did seem to promise much.

First she whispered him in corners when she came to the Theatre, telling him his poetry moved her heart, melted her legs and brought tears pricking to her eyelids; all of which put him in high hopes of further pricking in the shortest time possible. Second, she agreed to a secret meeting over the old Apothecary's shop, near to the Theatre at the sign of the Crocodile.

Now these Apothecaries did often let out their upper chambers for ladies to dance with their heels in the air, no doubt a better and healthier medicine for the gentlemen that partook of it than all the herbal remedies and specifics brewed below. The room where Will Shakespeare met with his Dark Beauty, brought there by her pandering and lecherous steward Nicholas (who perhaps got from the thought of his mistress's misbehaving such thin gruel of satisfaction as he could come by in no other way, lacking all hope of the feast itself), was furnished meagrely with little but a bed, a dusty mirror, and an hour glass to show, by its falling sand, when the time for Pleasure was over and the burden of marriage needs must be taken up again.

So Will Shakespeare stood there triumphant, and in front of him the boy Mary, the very points of her breast clear to him as her shirt unbuttoned, her belly and buttocks shaped in the tight small hose, thinking he had time and leisure to leave kissing and fondling and finally change the cod's head for the salmon's tail, when the cool self-regarder pushed him from her and uttered that word which is like a sentence of death to all upstanding Roger Codpieces. "Wait!"

"I must wait? Wait and die of waiting? Wait for the tomb and the worms to eat me!" Shakespeare looked at the hour glass and saw it was already three quarters empty.

"Not so long as *that*." She gave him a small hope, rather as they revive those on the rack with a gulp from the wine bottle.

"How long? Tell me how long?"

"You expect such a *quick* surrender?"

"I hope for it, or the besieger may die of starvation. Devil take it! You agreed to meet."

"To hear you woo. You woo so prettily."

"And win more prettily, I tell you." At which he held her hard to him and was given the freedom of her mouth, but for kissing. And then she escaped from his arms and he, knowing that true pleasure comes but with consent, stood inwardly raging.

"If I am worth winning, then I am worth waiting for. Poets are so impatient!"

"A poet," Will Shakespeare burst out, hating himself then for so feverishly loving her, "A noble poet! Once I planned murders, ghosts and battle scenes. Now it takes all my ingenuity to contrive a brief meeting between two characters in a druggist's shop!"

Mary smiled at him, feeling her power over the Poet. "But are they not fine, our love scenes, Will?"

"Lacking the right true end, an audience might find them something tedious."

The lower lip jutted again. This was not to her liking. "Tedious? Do you not love me, Will?"

"Love! Is that what's emptying my brain? My head's a huge empty chamber, echoing with your name, smelling of your perfume, with no other furniture! I sit alone . . ."

"Writing sonnets, I hope, in praise of my beauty!"

"Yes! The Devil take it. You are my only subject."

"No . . . No . . . Will. I know not how. I am not well today. It was the play. I was faint."

"There was too much blood," he allowed her.

"I am but faint-hearted for a boy."

"I told Dick Burbage. There was too much blood. They come for the words."

"For *your* words."

"Well, they best make the most of them. They are like to hear no more." Indeed, love had brought him a fever of hope, a despondency, a perpetual ache in the groin, a dry mouth, a sweating hand and a total inability to put pen to paper.

"Will. You have a play ready to deliver?"

"Talk not of plays! Talk rather to a lame man of jumping gates or to the deaf of music. I can no more deliver a play than I can father lion cubs or turn base metal into gold."

This wounded Mary in the only place she was truly vulnerable, in her vanity. She put her cheek against his chest and her thin arms about him. "Why, Will, do I not inspire you?"

"To a fever, madam! You raise my hopes, and let them die of longing." He had a hand cupped about her breast, and another possessing a small apple of buttock. But the sand in the hour glass was falling rapidly and Mary moved away, pouting her lower lip once more.

"What else would you write about?"

"I want to make a brave, jesting boy-girl for my new Comedy. But I think of you and my hand trembles, my palm sweats and I write another stanza to a dark beauty. My Lady Sorceress. You have taken all my powers."

His voice was so strong and his words so bitter she knew, I think, she must give him another sip of promise if he were to stay about her for the torturing. "Not *all* your powers, Will. You'll need save some – if you would capture my castle."

"My true potency is lost. I can no longer think of the stage. My heart is ever in the Apothecary's."

"It seems that I am not a medicine to agree with you." She was smiling now, perhaps because she saw the hour glass empty.

"If you would but give me a draught, I would be cured straight!"

"A draught?"

"A love potion, lady. Which I could drink straight from your sweet fountain."

Though this was promised it was in some dim and distant unimaginable future. "Oh, look, Will," she said as though she noticed the glass for the first time. "Our hour is finished. My Lord Justicer is expected home to dine."

"You cannot leave now!" It was a cry of agony and to stifle

it she kissed his mouth and whispered, "My Lord goes circuit soon. He leaves me lonely."

"So then?"

"I'll come to hear you woo. Prepare your loudest trumpets under my castle walls!" She slid from him like an eel and went to a closet and took out a dress she kept there hidden for when she came away from the Theatre. As she pulled it over her head she threw him another promise. "I think there's a traitor within me, Will. That may open to you." And as she went she gave him her final flattery, seeming jealous. "You have no other friend?" she asked him.

"I swear it!" he answered, and so forswore that Earl who was patiently watching the door of their secret meeting place from the other side of the street.

# 18

## Of Love Tokens, Serpents,
## And Other Secret Matters

So LET US take a new candle, pull the blanket further about
my knees (for decency's sake for writing of all this lechery
hath somewhat stirred my old marrow), touch pen for hair,
and begin this chapter with the meeting of two dogs in the
street near to the Judge's house in Middle Temple. One was
that same yapping lap-dog which took his exercise and fouled
all the courts of that lawyer's Paradise, at the end of a long
silk leash in the hands of the haughty Nicholas, and the other
was a fine aristocrat, a long legged elk-hound with a gold
studded collar led out for exercise by none other than my
Lord Southampton, who had Nicholas followed and knew
his household. And so these dogs, engaged as dogs will in
Spring-time in the mutual sniffing of backsides, were pushed
apart by Nicholas' long staff whilst he looked with disdain at
the owner of the impertinent elk-hound.

"Sir! Your dog is an annoyance to my dog!"

"And yours to mine," answered the Earl, in the voice of a
most superior lackey.

"This dog is dog to Mr. Justice Fleminge of the Queen's
Bench and his good lady, so have a care, sir, how you trifle
with him." Nicholas sounded like a lackey even nearer to
God.

"You best have a care, sir," Hal answered him. "This dog is
dog to the Earl of Southampton."

"You are my Lord Southampton's man, sir?" Nicholas sounded a trifle more respectful.

"No, sir, I am my own man : as this is my own dog."

At which Nicholas, seeing that he was in the presence of a Gentility high above that he had ever dreamed of, crooked the ancient hinges of his knees in a bow lower than he had ever managed before. "My Lord, I was hasty."

"It was understandable. You are concerned, no doubt, for the honour of the Judge's lap-dog. Is it a dog or a bitch, fellow?"

"My Lady's dog, my Lord, is without doubt a lady."

"And your Lord's Lady is what exactly? A boy-girl who faints away when the actors bleed? Come, man, I must have a crown's worth of conversation with you."

So the Earl invited the lackey to a bottle of fine Burgundy in a neighbouring tavern and from him gleaned much information about Mistress Mary Fleminge. So he learnt, which indeed he knew already, how that most respected lady went in breeches to the play, although Nicholas told him, as he knew to be a lie, that his mistress shunned the company of the players. "Low fellows, my Lord. Who keep their own company."

"We all keep our own company, unless we have you to guide us into better. Tell me, good Nigel . . ."

Southampton was corrected respectfully. "My name, my Lord, is Nicholas. In a merry mood my Lady will call me 'Old Nick'."

"The devil she will."

This was a jest which caused Nicholas near to choke with laughing, his life being just saved by another huge gulp of Burgundy. "Oh, my Lord has a merry wit! A merry and a pointed wit! My Lord and my Lady would have such jests together, such raillery!"

"Your lady enjoys a jest?"

"She will set me laughing at times, so my eyes are blind with tears. Hear, my Lord –" He seemed to be losing his breath again and again the wine saved him. "My Lady delights to play in the virginals. 'I must not play these now,' she tells me. 'Now I am a wife. I am no longer ... virginal.'"

"True, any jest may raise a laugh in a Judge's household."
The Earl sounded somewhat gloomy.

"But then she comes to me again, to say, 'Truth, my marriage has made no great difference. For my Lord Justice I may play the virginals still.'"

"Good Nicholas ..."

"My Lord?"

"Having seen your Lady as a boy, I have a great taste to see her as a Lady. But my Lord Justice keeps her close locked away?"

"Locks have keys."

"And guards have itching fingers." A heavy gold coin from the Earl's purse rolled across the table. Nicholas' hand took it as a heron's beak takes a fish.

"You might see her free and open. You might speak to her."

"Could a man be so blessed?"

"If my Lord were at my Lord Mayor's Banquet, where the Justices do dine with their ladies, your Lordship might see a spectacle!"

"Worth even turtle soup and the company of Judges?"

"As boy or girl, my Lord, my Lady is an enchantress. And we are all slaves who serve her."

And so it came about that Hal stifled his yawns to dine with the City Worthies and so was sat next, by the outlay of only a few more coins, the Learned Judge and his demure lady. Nibbling on a rind of cheese, and washing it down with something left over from an Old Communion, I must give their table talk the best of my imagination.

"'Tis not often we see an Earl in the City." The Judge raised his nose from the soup. "And I cannot remember the last time my Lord Mayor's Banquet was honoured by an Earl. Can you, wife?"

"Your wife?" Hal just glanced at the demure lady crumbling bread, her eyes cast down to her bubbies.

"Come, Mistress Fleminge, your respects now to my Lord Southampton."

"His Lordship does us too much honour," she whispered,

in that low voice which drove Shakespeare past the pitch of madness.

"Is she not pretty?" The learned Judge might have been showing off his silver. "Is she not fair? Are you not surprised, my Lord, so old a barncock gets so tender a chicken?"

"Nothing surprises me."

"I must go circuit tomorrow. It breaks my heart to leave my dear wife, Mary. But our country gaols are full to bursting. We must hang up some, my Lord, to make way for new felons."

"I suppose it's a pleasant enough way of visiting the country." Hal was sipping the Burgundy, which he found somewhat antique and musty.

"It's pleasant, my Lord. The lodgings are good and Sheriff's dinner excellent. Only it means leaving my sweet wife."

"No doubt she'll miss you sorely."

"Tell my Lord Southampton what you do, chuck, when I'm gone, for your diversion."

"I play upon the virginals." She spoke with a great modesty, and her old learned fool of a husband seemed unnaturally delighted.

"The virginals! Is it not a pretty chuck!"

"She also has the consolations of poetry?" At this Hal was pleased to see she had the grace to blush.

"Poetry! You have nought to do with poetry, chuck?"

"No, my Lord." Shakespeare would have wished her a better cause to lie in. The Judge was filled with deep satisfaction.

"It is the virginals with her," he boasted. "Never poetry. And soon you will have other cares, will you not, chuck? Other work to do." He whispered to Hal, drunk with pride, "She'll give me a son. A young babe! To a Queen's Bench Justicer. Something unknown in the annals of the court!"

"Before the next assize, I warrant." Hal smiled gracefully.

"Well, not so soon. Not quite so soon. There are some small problems. Of a medicinal nature. But with the help of Master Apothecary ..."

"With *his* help." Hal's face was straight, he was master of his smiling. "Let us hope devoutly all your troubles will soon be solved."

\* \* \*

I had done playing Lady Juliet that day but, being reluctant to quit the costume and, as I have said, more than half in love with my sweet self perfumed and skirted, I was still standing, alone in the tiring room in front of the mirror, when Will Shakespeare came to me, pale, tired and worn out with unperformed love, and interrupted my admiration of myself.

"Little Jack Rice!" he said as he saw both me and my reflection, "who knows how to get what he wants!"

"Haven't you learned that secret, Will?" At that time I thought he wanted for nothing, not coin nor fame certainly.

"No, faith, I have not!"

"What's the lost bone, that gives you that hungry dog expression?"

He then went to the mirror, where he saw but a gaunt playmaker. "Is my face read so easily?"

"I wager it's a couple of long bones that dance under a petticoat, with a pair of sweet thighs wrapped around them. Oh, for shame, will she not open to you, Will?" I was a pert boy then, and in my time of triumph I would say anything. It was the day I am now proudest of, the day he confided in me, as a friend almost, and not as a Poet to a monster of a boy player.

"I tell her my palms sweat from wanting her and that I am near to vomit, and it's my curse that I can do no work till she press the sheets with me."

I could not forbear to laugh at his style of wooing. "And with such charming speech, *still* she will not surrender?"

"How should I woo her, Jack?" Here he was, a very poet for lovers asking me for a lesson. I told him immediately

"Why, as Romeo wooed *me!* Say,

'Two of the fairest stars in all the heaven
Having some business do entreat your eyes
To twinkle in their spheres til they return.'

Have you said that to her?"

"Truly, Jack. I can write of lovers, but when we meet my tongue stumbles! It makes me angry and the anger chokes me!"

"Then let trinkets speak for you." It was a time, I saw, to be practical.

"I must buy silver? Or gold perhaps? My words are useless!" His words, which brought tears and laughter to so many hundreds, could not part a silly wench's legs for him.

I said, "You need a strong spell to move her."

"Have you one about you?" He was laughing as I went to the clothes basket and found that embroidered handkerchief my old mother clutched for witchcraft at the hour of death. By happy fortune it was worked with a serpent coiled in the shape of the letter 'S', which might be passed off as 'S' for Shakespeare.

"My grandmother was a gypsy. She worked this at full moon. You may say it was worked for your mother, who grew full-bellied just by looking into the eyes of the reptile."

"Would you believe that if you were she?" He sounded doubtful.

"I would believe just what I wanted. So will she, for sure she wants you secretly. Take it, there's a powerful magic in it."

He had no great faith in spells or witchcraft, thinking them mostly convenient for plays. But he took the handkerchief and seemed grateful for it. At the door he stopped and looked back at me, I remember, curiously. Perhaps he wondered how my success had changed me, curing, as success ever does, my more beastly faults of character.

"You would give me your treasure?" he asked.

I looked back at him and tried to tell him of my gratitude. "As you did me. When you parted me as your Lady Juliet."

That handkerchief ended in the hand of Hal Southampton,

and sitting opposite him at dinner Shakespeare saw him wipe
the grease from his lips with it. Later I will tell you how that
came about.

\*    \*    \*

"Look, I brought you a token."

"Will!" Mary Fleminge sounded filled with delight. As
he presented it to her there was a note of disappointment.
"Oh, a handkerchief." She did her best. "Beautifully
embroidered."

"A figure of an 'S', encircling a heart. A gypsy woman did
this work for my mother. 'S' for Shakespeare. It was a powerful spell."

"What spell?"

"The gypsy woman said that whoever wears this handkerchief shall be faithful in love. Look in the serpent's eyes."

Mary Fleminge was the sort of light lady to be much taken
with spells and witchcraft. She gazed into the eyes on poor
old mother's handkerchief. "I shall be faithful, Will. Faithful
until death."

"So long? Come, now. You'll see. It is a powerful magic."
And like a ship making for harbour he started to steer her
towards the bed. The hour glass in the apothecary's upper
room was still but half empty.

\*    \*    \*

In the garden of Southampton House Hal gave Nicholas
another, and far more costly, present for Mary Fleminge. It
was a fine jewelled brooch, worked in gold and silver filigree.
The serpent on it was 'S' shaped also, and had eyes of rubies,
'S' for Southampton, although Hal bade Nicholas, when he
gave it to Mary, tell her it was another 'S' for Shakespeare
and came from her most devoted poet.

"But as a stratagem, a merry stratagem, tell her Will Shakespeare sent her this. Your dark mistress, Nigel . . ."

"Nicholas."

"Nicholas is, it seems, a fountain of poetry. Where does she keep it?"

"Oh, as for that, my Lord," the old steward was smirking over the rich jewel. "There are private wells, and springs perhaps."

"Where a man fishing might catch a rhyme or two?"

\*　　\*　　\*

"Wait!" That dreadful word came again as Shakespeare had her by the bed and was about to bury Mary Fleminge with her face upwards. "Not yet."

"Presents! Tokens! Sonnets! Vows! And a sickness of desire near to death. What else must I do?"

"It's the bad time of the month for me. And my old Judge has been gone but a day. It is not seemly to be taken so soon. Wait till next week, Will. A little week. Is that so long?"

\*　　\*　　\*

When he dressed for Tybalt, Will was short and sharp with me, Lady Juliet. "There was no magic in it," he told me. "If your grandmother conceived, it was not the handkerchief. Nor, I swear, your grandfather either."

# 19

## Of An Act Of Friendship,
## Which Was Also
## An Act Of Darkness

NICHOLAS GAVE HIS Mistress the jewelled token which, being in the shape of an 'S', he said was from the Poet Shakespeare. "The blood and the Tomb must have pleased the groundlings," he told her. "The Player can spend so on trinkets."

"He would give me all. How can I thank him?" I believe Mary Fleminge said this as though she had no idea of what would please him most.

"This afternoon at Master Apothecary's you may show him some small trifle of gratitude. I would your sweet head knew how much honour is done you by the glittering 'S'."

"A poet's gift? What greater could there be?" She was holding the brooch to the bosom of her dress.

"Bless you, my lady! There be ranks far greater than poets. There be Gentlemen and Baronets, and Barons and Counts, Viscounts and even . . ."

"Even what?"

"There be Earls. Above all, madam. There be Earls!"

At which Mary laughed and as a cruel sport let him fix on her brooch, whereat the old steward trembled so at the touch of her bubbies that he pricked his finger and near ruined her dress with the blood from it. Later, I had it from another servant he went to a bawdy house to cure his lusts and caught a dose of the Spanish sickness: such a train of disaster did his Dark Mistress leave behind her.

\*   \*   \*

Now I must start to relate the cunning plot engineered by Hal of Southampton which led to the bitter quarrel between two friends, a dispute so terrible that the servants who witnessed it swore they were near to cutting each other to ribbons with the very carvers as they sat at dinner together. Truly it was an act by Hal of the greatest treachery towards his friend, and it was a treachery he meant to have discovered: but whether it was designed as a revenge for Will's infidelity, or to teach him his place, or as some terrible cure like blood-letting or the sawing off of a limb, I know not. But first let me set down the facts of that afternoon, which fell out to be a Thursday, when once again we played the Tragedy of the Star Crossed Romeo and Juliet. So, near as I can discover it fell out like this.

Two of the clock. Nicholas and his Mistress set out for the Apothecary's. Mary's little bubbies are swelling with pride, loaded with gold, silver and rubies and she is prepared at last to show her gratitude to Shakespeare. At the same hour the trumpet blows and we start the play with the Chorus setting our scene in fair Verona.

Two thirty of the Clock. Nicholas opens the door of the upstairs chamber over Master Apothecary's saying, "Are you hungry for love, my lady? The gentleman has a feast set out for you." He then leaves Mary, who goes into the dusty room, finds the bed curtains drawn; but hears a man, clearly much contented, whistling a catch behind them. She starts to take off her clothes, chattering the while.

"Your precious gift has unlocked my heart still. What can the castle do but surrender? You know, at times you seemed angry at loving me, Will. But now I know how dearly you treasure your Dark Love ..." And such like small talk.

Two thirty-five of the Clock. One I know not, some servant or lackey of Hal's as I now think, comes to the back of the Theatre and leaves word for Will Shakespeare that his Dark Beauty awaits him at the Crocodile.

Two thirty-six of the Clock. Naked and shivering a little

Mistress Mary Fleminge draws the bed curtains and leaps
into the warm bed with Hal, Earl of Southampton. One kiss
and she gasps her protests.

"You're not my poet!"

"Betwixt the sheets with you, my Lady, may not all men
be poets? Even so poor a man as I?"

"My Lord Southampton!" Stark naked in bed Mary
Fleminge still showed her nice respect for the Peerage of
England.

"You remember me. You had my token 'S'. Did you not read
it? 'S' for Southampton."

Mary laughs. She is still laughing at two forty-five when,
his lance readied and the mare eager, the Lord Hal began
the jousting.

Three of the Clock. Tybalt is slain, comes blood-stained
into the tiring room and I tell him of a message left by a
serving man that his Dark Lady awaits him at the Crocodile.
Life rushing back into him Tybalt runs from the Theatre, still
in his costume and wiping blood off with a towel, impatient
to meet his love.

Three fifteen of the Clock. Master Apothecary looks up
from his pounding of a mandrake to cure impotency, sees the
blood-stained Tybalt-Shakespeare run through his shop and
up the stairs and gives out a screech of horror as he remembers
how his upper room is occupied.

Three twenty of the Clock. Mary Fleminge is dressing, as
quickly as her fingers can find the buttons, between an Earl
swathed in a sheet and a Poet stained with pig's blood who
seem quite like to kill each other. When he told me of it
Shakespeare remembered some of her rattle.

"Poets! Peers! What do I need of them? I have a fine
house, I tell you. And a good man that loves me! And has
two fur gowns. And will hang up those who lie and trick and
deceive honest people, and can love nowhere but this old
dusty room that stinks of crocodile!" She was now dressed as
she turned on both of them. "Don't you come knocking at
my door either of you! For I shall tell my steward, 'Do not

open. They are rogues,' I shall tell him. 'Open again to no one, unless it be my good old Justicer come from hanging the likes of those two gentlemen.' Do you hear, my Lord? Hear you, Poet? I am at home to neither!"

# 20

## *Of A Quarrel, And A Parting*

YOUNG HERCULES, THE imp of a page, old Hercules now, who keeps the Flag Inn in Holborn and will thump a Bible on Sunday and his wife and all the chamber-maids the rest of the week, still remembers the silent dinner that night at Southampton House, where Earl and Poet sat at each side of the polished table and tore meat, chewed bones, cracked the claws of lobsters and spat out gristle as though they would rend and tear and spit out each other. And at the end Will Shakespeare stood up and the chair crashed behind him, and then the words were out with which they fought and wounded each other.

"Did I spy on my friend? Skulk down alleys? Peer through windows? Disguise myself to burrow into strange sheets? To poach my friend's fishpond and catch his trout?"

"You had betrayed me. Why did you so?"

"To be free a little."

"Were we not happy. When we hunted together?"

"A man has a right – to his unhappiness also."

"That's what she gave you? Unhappiness!"

"She gave me despair. Loneliness. An ache in the night that made me scream out in agony. No comfort . . ." The Poet looked so sad as he said this that the Earl was constrained to laugh.

"She told me – can this be true – That you had never . . . 'Captured her castle'. Her poetic phrase!" The laughter was

bubbling over, Hal could hold it no longer, and Shakespeare's
sad face and solemn words but increased his mirth.

"She spoke truth."

"Then why, by all that's sacred – that doleful countenance?
You have lost nothing!"

"No." The thought seemed to Shakespeare a great dis-
covery, and a distant sight of liberty. "I am free of her."

"You're yourself again!"

"I can go back to work. There are other subjects. Other
words. Besides her cursed beauty!"

Thinking he had his poet back Hal put a hand on Shakespeare's arm. "There speaks my Will. See, you have learned
what she is, a dark, heel-kicking drab of a wanton, I had to
teach you!"

And now those great unblinking eyes, the Poet's eyes, were
turned on Hal, and the voice was quiet as an accusation of
Treason. "*You?*"

Hal was merry again, ringing his golden bell and calling
for more wine. "Just as I have taught you to sit for a canter
and wipe your mouth before drinking and not swear oaths
when there were ladies present. Faith, little poet, your face
when I had you brought to the bedroom! I need must laugh."

"You had me brought?"

"How else could I show you what she was, in truth?"

"You schemed to lie with her, you had me brought?"

"For your own good, Will. You've learnt your lesson like
an apt pupil."

At which it seems Shakespeare left the dining chamber
and went to the library, returning with his hand full of those
poems rhymed as sonnets, which were writ to ever prove the
Poet's love and make the Earl immortal. Hal looked and
wondered why Shakespeare had brought them, but said
nothing.

"Your one moment of glory, wasn't it, Lord Envious? Did
you feel grand and triumphant when you passed for Will
Shakespeare? As well you weren't challenged for a rhyme,
else had all been discovered."

"You may presume too far." Try as he would Hal sounded

like a Master of the Hunt, rebuking a favoured groom. And it was this voice which stung Shakespeare to his great fury.

"Oh, there he speaks, My Lord Arrogant! What, does the groom complain when my Lord confers his favours on the lackey's mistress? Whip him in the kennels with the thieving cook and pert page! What am I? Your plaything! My Lord Charmouth has a clockwork song-bird, but the Earl of Southampton has a real live poet who can sing all night without winding."

"You have not sung much of late. But now I have cured you of your sickness. You may finish these verses that are to be my monument. 'To me fair friend you never shall be old . . .' How does the line go?"

Shakespeare moved with the handful of papers towards the great crackling fire of perfumed logs. "The line goes," he said quietly, "into the fire!"

Then Hal saw all the years after his death about to crumble to ashes. He held Shakespeare, and his were the stronger arms, although the poet's words still fought for him.

"Look in the mirror now. Watch yourself grow creased and old! My verses shan't keep you young, for no one shall read them! Men will forget the old Earl who once knew a poet."

"No, Will. Fool, Will, no." Hal was ever wrestling to keep his poems from the fire.

"Why not?"

"They are too fine." And so Hal said something stronger than all the pulling and scuffling, words which drove Shakespeare to leave the fire, fold his sonnets and put them into the breast of his doublet.

"True. You say true."

"Leave me my future. And forget the past," said Hal, thinking he was now on a winning streak.

"The past is here. The past is with us always."

So Hal smiled and went back to the table, where Rhenish wine was being poured by Hercules. "Shall we ride into the country tomorrow? Shall we go hunting, Will?"

"You have hunted, my Lord, in my forest. From this time

you must hunt alone." There was a chill in Shakespeare's
voice as he turned to the door.

"Will. Will, you're not to go!" Hal seemed not to believe
what he was seeing. "Where will you be, without a Lord to
befriend you?"

"Where I was, when all my friends were players."

Hal was taking a glass of wine and still seemed full of
confidence. "Scribbling for the next half crown. Playing in ale
houses and sleeping in carts. A poor player! I made you
a gentleman, almost." His glass was at his lips as he heard
Shakespeare's answer.

"Then let me stop you. Before the task is completed."

Hal was amazed when he saw the door was open. "You're
not to go, Will!" His eyes were full of tears and his voice
was high and furious as, when a child, he had been whipped,
or had a toy taken from him. "Will. You are not to go!"

But the door banged shut. His Private Poet was gone.

*　　*　　*

Hercules told me that when Shakespeare ran down the great
staircase of Southampton House he was scowling with rage,
but as soon as he was let out of the door he stopped, took
breath, and burst out laughing. I think now he had the first
inkling of the best breeches role he ever made for me, that
of fair Rosalind in the Forest of Arden who said of love, if
I can remember how it ran exactly (it is strange and merciful
that I can call to mind most of what I learnt as a boy-girl
player, but have quite forgot our Rector's rebuke over the
matter of the unscrubbed step yesterday, or my last week's
bill for ale, owing to Hercules), Rosalind's opinion of man's
passion, went thus, as I remember it. "Love is merely a
madness, and I tell you deserves as well a dark house and
a whip as madmen do; and the reason why they are not so
punished and cured is, that the lunacy is so ordinary that the
whippers are in love too."

In that play I was to cure a man of the mad-sickness of love
by playing, as Shakespeare wrote, "effeminate, changeable,

lying and liking, proud, fantastical, apish, shallow, inconstant, full of tears, full of smiles, for every passion something, for no passion truly anything, as boys and women are for the most part, cattle of this colour". I was then a boy pretending to be a girl, pretending to be a boy. In short I was to enact that Dark Lady of whom he never was, I now think, perfectly cured.

# Part Four

## "THE LOVED BOY"

"And jealous Oberon would have the
   child
Knight of his train to trace the forests
   wild;
But she perforce withholds the loved
   boy."
> A Midsummer Night's Dream.

# 21

## *Of Witches, Sorcery*
## *And Mistress Anne Shakespeare*

"The story is of a wood near Athens. There is a quarrel brewing between King Oberon of the Faery Land and Titania his Queen, a matter of dispute concerning a little changeling child. A loved boy."

I picture the poet Shakespeare, on one of his none too frequent visits to Stratford, holding a horn spoon in one hand, trying to beguile his little son Hamnet, his rascal whom he had told Kit Marlowe he loved or nothing in the world, to take some thin mutton stew which Mistress Anne had prepared for dinner. And as he listened to the tale of the play he had then in hand, young Hamnet so far gratified his father as to take the spoon and eat stew while he listened.

"Well. King Oberon would have the child though his Queen laid claim to it. And at their falling out there was chaos and dissension in Faery Land. Winter changed places with Summer. Spring came in hot after Autumn. The green corn rotted in the snow and there was seen ice on the roses."

Anne, waiting to clear the table, looked at the two menfolk in her family with contempt. "Still he's sullen. Husband, you waste your breath."

And the two girls complained. Judith said, "Father never tells *me* stories," and Susanna told her, "It's because you eat too easily."

"If I stopped eating, would he tell me one, would he?"

"The boy was ever his father's favourite." Anne piled their

bowls as noisily as she could and made a great clanking with
the beer mugs. "The more so since he went mulish. Are we
to wait all night or will the Queen of the Faeries wash the
pots for us?"

The truth of the matter was, not only was Hamnet hard
to feed, he had not spoken one word for the six months past.
No one in Stratford had heard him utter, and he spoke not to
his mother, nor his sisters nor, and this went near to breaking
Shakespeare's heart, to his father when he visited him, and
though he listened, his eyes wide with wonder, to all that
strange, fantastical tale of King Oberon and Queen Titania,
he had not a word to say to it. So the poet's son, who of all
son's in the world should have been eloquent, was silent.

*       *       *

There were it seems a great many witches in the Shire of
Warwick. Some were white witches who did little but heal
cuts and bruises and help old ladies sewing to find lost
thimbles. But there were many black witches, who had the
power to fly through the air riding on a staff, or to withstand
pain after the swallowing of a King Bee, which made it
impossible to rack or torture them to any satisfaction. These
were the Beldams, usually with a gammy leg, a bearded
chin, a warty hand and a skinny finger, who washed neither
above the waist nor below it so it needed a powerful charm
(such as an orange stuck with cloves held under the nostrils)
to come anywhere near them.

Now there was a certain Beldam Trot who lived in a hut
on a piece of waste ground near to Shakespeare's house in
Stratford. As the Poet was now a man of some property, earning sometimes the like of two hundred pounds in one year,
and sending much of it home to his family, and as Anne kept
the house and children scrubbed and the garden tidy, any
foul-smelling old woman who slept in rags under a roof of
wattles, whose mangy dog howled all night prancing at the
end of a rope, who stewed up rabbits and small voles in a
cooking pot under the stars, must have seemed a pestilence

sent direct by the Devil. So Beldam Trot was a witch to Anne, as full of sin as was the Dark Lady, when she came to learn of her existence.

The children knew for certain there were Familiars, Frogs and Rattle Snakes kept in the old crone's hut, as well as wax dolls of various old gentlemen that planned Mother Trot's burning, which she often stuck with pins and so caused howls of pain in these old Worthies' bedrooms. But the chief Nuisance was the hag's tied-up black dog which howled like all the ghosts in the churchyard. So one night young Hamnet Shakespeare went out with a meat knife and cut through the rope. The cur was off like a bat from Hell into the neighbouring Shire of Oxford, and Hamnet was, of course, cursed by the Beldam and ever since fell silent.

"I stand astonished," Shakespeare said to his wife when she told him of it. "You a God-fearing woman, that has some little learning too. You scratch your head like a yokel and prattle of Beldams."

Their neighbours Judith and Hamnet Sadler were to supper that night, and Anne didn't care to be rebuked in front of them as well as in the presence of her children. "At least I don't tell faery tales at dinner," she answered, her eyes appealing to the sensible Sadlers.

"That is my playmaking. Not my superstition."

"He speaks not to either, for all your playmaking."

"Have you thought of this, the boy stays silent for he has nothing to say in this house."

"His own home! Ay, he has nothing to say to us."

"Perhaps you say nothing, to engage his interest." I think Shakespeare found life so dull then at Stratford that he was glad of the drama of this quarrel. Certainly young Hamnet was watching it as if he were sitting at a play. And Anne's rage was now growing to a voice Ned Alleyn might have envied.

"What? I must engage his Lordship's interest! I must curtsey low to the Almighty Infant and say, 'I am your mother, would you please talk to me.' Susanna, be a good girl

now, Susanna. Put on the children's nightgowns. Take them
up to bed . . ."

"Why should he talk? Here the talk is all of making pre-
serves or gossip about the neighbours."

"They shouldn't hear their parents tussle so," said Judith
Sadler, and persuaded Susanna to take the younger children
up to bed!"

"Goodnight, my son. We'll have the rest of that tale tomorrow." Shakespeare kissed his boy, who answered nothing,
and when Hamnet had gone he looked after him. "I wonder
he has the strength to speak at all!" Shakespeare filled his
mug and drank beer. "That weak stew of watery muttons;
it's not enough for a puppy-dog to yelp on, let alone make a
boy talk!"

"That weak stew!" Anne was outraged.

"So weak it had to be helped from the cauldron. A boy
must be fed well to be cheerful and hearty. Could he not be
fattened up for conversation? Is there nothing here to buy
a pound of beef or a cony? What do you do with all I send
from London?"

Whereat the fuming Anne dragged down a box from a
shelf, unlocked it, and showed a great winking, glittering
mass of coin, product of much ink and hard-learned acting.
She showed it off, triumphant. "There's your money!"

"You never spend it." The poet who earned it was looking
at the money, almost with disgust.

"She's still a good manager, neighbour William. A good
housewife and careful manager." Mistress Judith Sadler
rallied to the side of economy.

"Sure, any housewife can manage a graveyard, where the
corpses need no dinner provided."

"Your children are fat and hearty." Honest Hamnet Sadler
was thinking that London life had not improved his neighbour, and wondering how a one-time horse-minding capon-
stealer should have become so particular about his dinner.

"Then must the citizens of Stratford show great charity to
starving infants."

"Neighbour Anne doesn't feed them fanciful. But there's

good solid fare in this house and plenty of it. Is there not, husband?" Judith Sadler was now the champion of all her sex.

"Ay. That there is, wife." Hamnet was still at a big round cheese, paring at it with his knife, and spoke with his mouth full.

"Your son's not starving, William! And not speaking either," Anne said, and banged the box of money shut.

"He'll speak to me," his father told her, "when he knows all I have in store for him."

\* \* \*

If, in the scene here pictured, drawn as it is from Shakespeare's memory when he told me of it and my own imaginings, together with such talk as I once had with the honest Hamnet Sadler over a pint of bastard ale when I played at Stratford, Mistress Anne is shown as a cold, sour woman and tyrannical, or even as that She-Dragon her husband sometimes called her, I do not think I am doing her justice. For Anne, like all women, no doubt, was a creature of contradictions. She was still handsome and had been beautiful, and as her first encounter with the boy Shakespeare showed, when she took him to help her pick primroses on the long walk to Shottery and was scarce into the woods before she nigh pulled the breeches off him and was on her back on a mossy hillock with her heels dancing in the air, she was at heart a jolly and gamesome woman, capable of great and glorious frivolity. But Will Shakespeare's desertion of her, for his long absences can only be called such, had forced the man out of those petticoats. She had to play husband as well as wife, father as well as mother, and she stifled and strangled that light woman within her for fear she could not else keep the children obedient, or her house so clean, scrubbed and well appointed. And this I believe: due to their long partings Anne and William, even on his rare visits, had fallen out of that habit of mutual entertainment when two people be so intent on the act of husbandry in the world of the wide bed, that all grievances and disputes are forgotten and the next day is spent in memory of a fine fondling and never on quarrels. So Anne was such a woman as must ever be damping down the fires of her true nature, and there is no doubt that such a work put her into an ill-humour whenever her husband came to visit; and the dispute and wrangling over that boy who seemed to be growing as contrary and stubborn as his poet father did little to mend her temper.

Whilst on this visit husband and wife once again took the long walk to Shottery, but, instead of pressing the mossy banks, they stalked with raised voices which caused the rooks to clatter startled in the tree tops, and the rabbits to hide in their burrows.

"Hamnet. A butcher!" Shakespeare was in a high rage, not having heard of the suggestion before.

"Neighbour Sadler has the lease of a shop in Friday Street. Our boy can be apprenticed . . ."

"I'll not have it!"

"Cutting carcasses he'll have no need for speech-making."

"Never!" Shakespeare vowed.

"Why not? Your father was a glove-maker. Why not your son a butcher? Though you have no trade."

"No trade? I have a profession – "

"Which keeps you from home at night, in the foul company of light women and mountebanks."

"A profession that brought us all to the Queen's Court at Michaelmas to give my comedy!" He was now a Courtier, and had put into the College of Heralds for a family Coat of Arms. He was not to be father to a butcher-boy.

"Oh, butchers come to Court too, to deliver pig's meat and chitterlings." Anne could joke a little still, though most jests had gone sour with her.

Shakespeare took her arm and under the beeches, among the primroses, in a wood near Stratford where they had once gone courting, he gave her the benefit of an oration. "Listen to me, wife," he said. "There are men in London that have gathered pearls on the shores of the Bermudas. There are doctors that have looked through a glass and counted the stars. There are clowns to make a man laugh and poets, so many of us poets, to make him weep. There is money and preferment for the wise and cunning. Is there to be none of this for Hamnet?"

"Who can give it to him?"

"Why, I can if I take him to London."

Anne thought a little. Then she said quietly, "When do you go back?"

"Tomorrow."

So she gave him her answer, a reply far more shocking and outrageous than any denial. "Very well. Take him tomorrow!"

Shakespeare was like those sinners offered immediate reformation; sure he wanted to be saved, but not quite yet. "I meant. When he has grown a little."

"When he has grown a little he'll be sawing carcasses. Take him now!" Anne's voice was clear and determined.

"It may not be convenient."

"Has it been convenient for me? So many years, a boy without a father."

"I have a play in the writing. A comedy of country people." He knew the excuse sounded but lame, after his protestations of love for Hamnet.

"You, you love the boy so! Will you not take him with you? Or are you content to leave him to his silences?"

So this was an argument Anne won. About dawn the next day horses were saddled and Anne handed over Hamnet and his bundle to her husband.

"Two shirts I have put in. And a bottle of syrup for his cough."

"I'll buy shirts in London. Say goodbye to your mother, Hamnet."

The boy moved to her silently, but Anne turned away.

"You are your father's boy now," she said. "Seemingly I can do no more for you."

# 22

## Of How The Loved Boy
## Was Took To Faery Land

As HE MADE his journeys betwixt Stratford and London Shakespeare was used to spend a night at a wine house called the Taverne at the sign of the Bush in the Cornmarket of Oxford. The landlord there was one John Davenant, whose wife Mistress Davenant was of great beauty and regarded Shakespeare as a most favoured client, so favoured in fact that eventually she gave birth to that Sir William Davenant who was himself a versifier, capable of such a line as "Lovers whose priests all poets are", which was wondered at as there had, till then, never been a sign of poetry in the good Taverner's family. Such advantage can an Inn reap but by serving a customer like Shakespeare.

So the Poet arrived with his son born on the right side of the blanket, but the loved boy would eat little of the fine pastries and roasts set before him, and only demolished a custard.

"The boy is nervous," the father explained to the landlady, who looked, in a crisp white apron, smiling in the light from the fire, as fragrant and zestful as her own partridge pie. "He still fears his sainted mother may come after us on a broomstick."

Mistress Davenant remembered when Will Shakespeare first ran away to London, and stopped at the back door of the Taverne to beg a crust and a drink of water. She had loved him a little then, and more so after more stops, and more journeyings. But that night Hamnet was restless, he was staring wide-eyed at the candle when Shakespeare came up to bed. The Poet knelt beside his son and asked gently, "Do you have bad dreams, boy?"

There was still no answer, so Shakespeare promised him all he had power to give. "Listen, Hamnet. Tomorrow we leave here and ride for London. There you may see fire-eaters and jugglers and bears in the bear-pit, and perhaps the Queen at Court with all her fine Lords and Ladies gathered round her. You want to see that, don't you, Hamnet?"

Then there came a tap on the door, it opened a chink and in looked Mistress Davenant, warm and rosy in her shift. Shakespeare was for moving to her but he felt the boy's grip on his sleeve. "The boy fears dreams," he whispered reluctantly. "I must stay with him."

"You lie with him always?"

"Well, not always perhaps. Give you goodnight, Mistress Davenant."

The door closed and, resigned, the father climbed into bed beside the son who now slept peacefully.

\* \* \*

*The Dream of a Midsummer Night*, as I think we titled it, was a play the author had a great difficulty in finishing. We had certain scenes about Lovers and Faeries, but the comical pantomime of the rude mechanicals to which he promised to give birth was slow in its gestation. However, he promised Hamnet a sight of the Queen at Court, and as he could not then command Queen Elizabeth, Hamnet must make do with Queen Titania, who being young Jack Rice in a skirt of moonshine and a crown of silvery cobwebs (fishnet and painted cottons with much glass jewellery, twisted wire and shimmering satins) was yet more Magically Majestical than ever the Great Virgin herself. (One may say that now; time was when you might stand in the pillory for suggesting old Vanity could not raise men upshooting just by passing in procession.)

So he sent word before and we were all ranged in paint and costumes on the stage when Shakespeare led his son to the door of the Theatre.

"Just as I told you, Hamnet. The Queen's Court is here with all her fine Lords and Ladies. Shall we go in? Her Majesty knows me well."

So was Hamnet led into the wooden O of the Theatre, and the first he saw was the King and Queen of Faeryland, surrounded by a fine collection of mortals and immortals. And as the reigning Monarch I gave the boy a fine roust of welcome, seizing a sword from King Oberon-Burbage wherewith to dub him a Knight of the Theatre.

"Hamnet Shakespeare," I cried in falsetto. "You are welcome to our Court. You shall be one of us, entitled to beef on Thursdays, pigeon pie Tuesdays and to be drunk head over heels on strong waters Saturday night!" So then I touched the boy's shoulder with the sword. "Arise, Sir Hamnet! I call for a loving cup of strong ale for Sir Hamnet Shakespeare!"

Then behold an Ass with a man's legs (Will Kempe as Bully Bottom) came out of the tiring room with mugs of ale and we all drank to the health and happiness of this dumbstruck boy.

"Be not afeared," said Sam Crosse to the boy. "This is no Queen of Faeryland."

"Only the Queen of Shoreditch," said the spiteful Cooke. "Lift its petticoat and you may see its little carrot."

"They are but players," Shakespeare assured him. "It's the tale I told you, of the enchanted forest. This is Dick Burbage, our King Oberon . . ." So he began the introductions, and one by one we tried if we could not set this child's mind at rest and charm it into speech.

Burbage was effusive. "Welcome, dear Heart. For shame, Will! What a little farmyard doublet your boy has on. He shall to my tailor. We may find something in watered silk with a velvet small hose. Would that not do bravely for you, boy?"

But Hamnet said nothing, and his father took him on. "Hemminge and Condell, who play two lovers and count the takings."

Hemminge asked cheerfully, "Will you join the family? Give you another three inches and we'll make you a waiting lady or a heroine's friend."

"Not for your starving wages. My son comes for a share as a poet. Sam Crosse, our Duke Theseus."

At which Sam Crosse brought out a little cage with a bright-eyed bird hopping in it. "I trapped you a little singing bird, Hamnet; a London thrush."

Hamnet took the caged bird and seemed pleased to do so, but gave no answer. Nor did he speak when Will Kempe in his ass's head danced a burgomask light and strong and insolent as only he could dance it, while we played to him on reed and tabor. When it was over Hamnet looked most serious but still did not speak.

"Master Hamnet," said Burbage, after we had all done our best, "you are welcome to our company. Come, hearts. Let us rehearse. A chair! Put a chair for Master Hamnet."

A chair was set and Hamnet sat there attentive whilst Burbage and I rehearsed. The King and Queen of Faeryland accused each other of dalliance and pastimes with others, and the boy Hamnet listened as though it were the most natural thing in the world.

Burbage berated me,

"For shame how canst thou thus, Titania,
  Glance at my credit with Hippolyta
  Knowing I know thy love to Theseus?
  Didst thou not lead him through the darkening night?"

"No, Dick! *Glimmering!*" Shakespeare was among us, arguing, as usual, over a single word.

"What?"

"Through the *glimmering* night. You said 'darkening'."

Burbage considered the matter and said, "Darkening is the better!"

"Darkening is dull as matrimony! The word is *glimmering.*"

"Nonsense! How can a night glimmer?" Burbage was a good business man and a great actor, but no poet.

"Are you always drunk abed? Have you never seen moonlight?"

"Calm you, dear heart. For your sake we will try 'glimmering'." Burbage was a man, also, of sweet kindness and true gentility.

The argument won, Shakespeare looked at the stool and, lo and behold it was empty. He searched the Theatre and found, in the tiring room, a child in a velvet cloak, wearing the mask of a gaping skull and a King's crown. He kissed Hamnet, disrobed him and took him to his lodgings with the sharp-nosed Mother Parker of Bishopsgate. There he had a bedchamber and a writing room where hung maps and pictures and there were globes and swords, books and bottles such as Kit Marlowe once had littering his chamber. The caged thrush was hung in the bedchamber. Mother Parker, who trusted not actors, particularly those with children, was placated with a sovereign and sent out to buy "the biggest custard in London". Shakespeare opened a bottle of white Bavarian and Hamnet was content to take a sip out of his father's glass.

"I bid you welcome, Hamnet, to the world of men. Here shall we be safe from all ladies." That was their toast, as they began life together, the poet and the child.

# 23

## *Of A Visit To A Married Earl*

JUST AS NO love lasts for ever, at least without change, so no quarrel can be kept alight indefinitely, it must die down to a tolerance, out of which, Phoenix-like, a new friendship, even a new love, may be born. So it was with Shakespeare and Hal of Southampton. They met once by chance, at a play, and then at an Inn, and then rode out into the country together to see some gypsies wrestling, and came back to all outward showing as close as ever; although there were some wounds, I must suppose, in both their hearts which neither would care to have reopened. But Will Shakespeare was set on being a sharer of my Lord Chamberlain's Company of Actors, under whose patronage we all now were. Times had changed since the day when a share in a cry of players might be bought for a handful of florins or a play, and Hal gave his friend as much, I have heard, as a thousand pounds to buy his share. I do not think at all that he was buying friendship, but sure it's easier for men of wealth and station to pay for their infidelities.

Neither did his outrage at the Dark Mary Fleminge last for ever: Shakespeare came by her house one night masked with music, and being by now prosperous threw in her window a trinket she could not ignore. So, often on her way to Church she would stop by his lodgings. It was strange that having been once tumbled by the Great Earl of Southampton she would open now so easily to his friend. He still desired

her passionately, but having on each visit buried her face
upwards, he found he could almost dislike her and so his
writings were not long interrupted. Sometimes he felt a great
disgust at lust with so little love in it, and wrote of such
expense of spirit in those poems which were to bring so much
trouble to him.

But to return to Hal Southampton. That their friendship
was strong still, but that it was altered, are both proved by
the fact that Poet and Peer continued to meet after Elizabeth
Vernon, one of the Queen's Ladies, had most secretly married
her lover and the father of her child and become the new,
penniless, pretty enough but somewhat ordinary Countess of
Southampton. When Will asked his friend why he had married her Hal threw back his head, threw in a glass of cold
white wine and laughed.

"The poor fool was so sick for love of me. And it's a pretty
fool, is it not, having something of your boy-girl heroines
about her? And she had my child kicking inside of her. But
more than all, she was the only Court lady found time to
flatter me." He paused for a moment to acknowledge his
reflection in a mirror.

"Small wonder she got you then, my Lord Looking-Glass,"
Shakespeare told him.

"None of the other Maids of Honour would tell me I was
beautiful. They kept all their compliments for Her Almighty
Virgin Majesty, who must have fifty poems in praise of her
antique nose before she will take her breakfast!"

It is sure Hal married not out of ambition, for on hearing
of the match the "Almighty Virgin" sent the groom to cool
his heels a month in the Tower.

So, seeking to show his son some noble company, Shakespeare took Hamnet to Southampton House. As you will
judge the visit was not a marked success. As Hercules told
me, "When an old friend meets a new wife you may look out
for broken glasses." He was wise as a page boy. With the
years, his wisdom is somewhat abated.

At dinner the Earl's new Countess was gracious to the poet.

"Master Shakespeare," she said, "my Lord has told me all you did in the days he was a bachelor."

"What, *all*, my Lady?" This news surprised Shakespeare.

"When you started up from the country to write plays, did you ever dream you might sit at an Earl's table?" the Countess asked him.

"I knew the work would be hard. But I did not guess at all the perils of the Theatre, Lady."

Her Ladyship was apparently well satisfied by the answer. "My Lord told me, he was a great comfort to you, in all your troubles."

"He told you that?"

"And how he would sit in the Great Library at Tichfield and give you tales and verses to make up into plays."

"Your Lord was ever a great contriver of plots."

Even the shameless Hal now had the grace to look ashamed. "Bess, you exaggerate! I told you I had helped our poet. I helped you a little, didn't I, Will?"

"Not a whit!" Shakespeare turned to the Countess. "He took away my spur to playmaking."

"Your spur? You mean your inspiration?"

"No, Lady. I mean my hunger. I ever eat too well at my Lord Indulgent's table."

Hal was now delighted to be put into a position to say, "Take away the roast goose, Hercules. Else we lose another tragedy."

A nurse came in with a bundle of fine lace which yelled most prodigiously, it was Hal's daughter Penelope.

"What do you want of us, Will?" Hal asked Shakespeare, almost serious.

"Want? I came from friendship – and to show my boy the wonders of the world."

"What are they?"

"The bear-pit at Shoreditch, the two-headed woman of Hounslow and the married Earl of Southampton House."

"Should such wonders make the boy speechless?" Hal said as his wife cooed over the screeching baby.

Hamnet, who had said not a word all through dinner, tucked into the custard.

"I hope, Hal, they will make him speak." Shakespeare seemed near despair, but Hal, as usual, laughed at him and called over his baby's yawlings, "What miracle is there, do you think, might strike *my* bratling dumb?"

\* \* \*

Hamnet was bored, unoccupied, and shunning the company of those elders who spoke not to him, for in truth he spoke not to them, he wandered up the great staircase and gazed at the fine paintings of the Southampton ancestors. Hal was out showing Will Shakespeare the stables, and, as the Spring wind was sneeping, sent Hercules in to fetch his furred cloak. So Hercules came down the stairs and found a child of his own age, sullen, silent, who still gave himself the airs of a guest. Hercules set about to explain the pictures.

"That's my master's grandfather," he said, as if introducing his own family. "The great Lord Montecute. And that was the Countess. His beautiful mother. And Lord Burghley, Lord High Treasurer of the Realm and my Earl Master's Guardian. Those are our arms, quartered with those of Beaulieu. Does it not strike wonder in your heart, yokel, to see such grandeur here?"

But taunted as he was Hamnet did not give the page the pleasure of an answer.

"Why don't you speak, yokel? What do you do in the country? Trade grunts with the pigs and moo to the cattle? Let me instruct you. In a Lord's house we give a civil 'good day'. In English."

Once again Hamnet gave Hercules the benefit of his silence.

"All right. Grunt you goodbye, Master Swineherd. I'll not be troubled with you!"

But Hercules was troubled, by a punch in the eye and a hand under his throat and then, in a tumble of arms and legs the two boys, the poet's son and the page boy, were rolling arse over crown down the stairs, fighting like boys ever will, in the first real sign of liveliness young Hamnet had given so far.

In the stables, where Hal was looking over a new mare he had a mind to buy, Shakespeare tried to explain to his friend all he wanted for his son.

"All knowledge must be open to him. I want him to love all my friends and laugh at my comedies. He will cry at all my plays tragical. And now he shall be a gentleman."

"Now?" Hal left his inspection of a fetlock to look wonderingly at his friend.

"I have petitioned the College of Heralds, that we may have a Coat of Arms for our family." Shakespeare had the grace to sound half-ashamed, and Hal had not the grace to keep from laughing.

"William! My pure poet! Who would lord it over his aristocratic patron with nothing but his talent to boast of and that mightily. *You* seek a stamp for your silver, like a dull country Knight or a bone-headed Baronet?"

"It's well, for the boy to have it." William was quick with his excuses.

"What are the arms, William? Two crossed pens and a dark lady rampant? Do you still have her – the one I stole from you?"

"Make merry. My Lord Mock-Anything."

"Blow trumpets!" Hal imitated a Herald. "Make way there. For Lord William of the Bedchamber! One step more and you'll be my equal. Worthy of the axe on Tower Hill. Quite above being hanged like a beastly commoner." He shivered, not I'm sure in premonition of his terrible sentence, but only from the icy March wind. "Are we to freeze to death? Hercules! Where's that boy with my furs?"

And then Hercules appeared, with a black eye, a bloody nose and torn livery. And near to him as a friend, similarly torn and bloodied, was the quiet lad, Hamnet Shakespeare.

\*     \*     \*

Walking home through certain foul and narrow streets Shakespeare, moved at last to anger at such behaving in his friend's house, berated his loved son.

"There are certain things, Hamnet, you don't do when you're to dinner with an Earl." So he gave Hamnet his lesson in gentility. "You don't push the venison pastry aside and fall on the custards like a starving animal. You don't indulge in fisticuffs with the servants. This above all – when my Lord speaks to you, you do return some answer. Do you hear me, Hamnet? Do you hear your father, boy?"

Hamnet's silence seemed like a perpetual rebuke. Shakespeare knelt and did what I would have done long before. He knelt and shook the child. "In sweet Christ's name, Hamnet! I beg you, speak to me!"

Matters then took place with a startling rapidity. There was, lying against a staircase in the mud and offal of that same street a "Samaritan", that is to say one who feigned injury so he might stab and foist the purses of those who were fool enough to help him. This Samaritan called out, "Mercy! Help me, kind sir. I am wounded." And Will Shakespeare, who as a native of London streets should have known better, was fool enough to cross and do so. Whereat the sturdy foist plunged an iron into Shakespeare's arm and ran off the better for a heavy purse of gold, and the Poet sank into the Samaritan's place, the poorer by a good goblet of blood. Indeed, the world seemed somewhat misty as he looked up into the face of Hamnet, bending over him like a nurse.

"I should have stopped you going to him, Father," said Hamnet. "You may not trust such people."

It is to be noted that when at last the child spoke it was to say something entirely sensible. There was much of his mother in him.

# 24

## Of Shakespeare's Second Marriage

Now it was Hamnet's turn to feed his father broth with a spoon, while Shakespeare lay at his lodging recovering from his wound and we still waited for him to write the comic pantomime of the Rude Mechanicals. Whenever Dick Burbage asked him for it he said, "My boy does prattle so. Why, last night we heard midnight strike and still we were talking."

No doubt it is natural for a man to love his son, whom he sees in vanity as the little mirror of himself, a part of him to send out into the dark years to come, a surer way to cheat mortality than even poetry or the hope of Heaven. (I put this down in secret with only the vestry mice for company. May I not speak as I think?) Having so much neglected him, and keenly regretting his guilt in that regard, Shakespeare was bound to love his Hamnet above the common run of fathers. Now by some seeming miracle the boy spoke to him again and he was in a very honeymoon of affection and indeed hung on the child's words, more as if he were a lover than a son.

One day he asked the boy, "What was that long silence, eh? What was it, my Lord Secret?"

"It was an oath. I swore an oath."

"What?"

"Not to speak until you came back to me, father. I swore it by moonlight and pricked my finger. It was a good oath and effective."

"Did you want me then, so much?"

"Out of the love I bore you, sir. As my own Father."

Shakespeare laughed; he was sure that there was no one, in the whole world, as like to him as this boy. "The house was dull, eh, Hamnet? By Heaven, I found it dull."

"My mother, and my sisters, I don't think well understand your stories, sir." Hamnet could not have said anything to please his father more.

"No. No, Hamnet. I don't think so either."

"So, well, I swore the oath."

"But when I brought you with me, still you were silent." Shakespeare was still puzzled a little.

"I was not sure. I thought you'd tire of me, sir. And send me back."

"Never! You know well, Hamnet. I'll never send you away." He swore an oath and meant it.

"Not if *he* asks you?"

"Who's *he*?"

"The man in silver clothes."

In truth, the man in silver clothes, Hal of Southampton, came to visit the sick, together with Hercules bearing codling pie and a dozen bottles of Bavarian. When he was come Hamnet went into the bedchamber to talk to the thrush they had named Puck, after the Robin Goodfellow in the play. And Hal confessed that his marriage, which had seemed to him an adventure when it angered the Queen and led him to the Tower, was more of a prison now he was out of it.

"My son has spoken!" Shakespeare had only one thought and that was not of his friend's marriage. "He has spoken to me at last."

"What did he say?" Hal seemed not to think this fact the eighth wonder of the world. "Anything of interest? We must escape together, Will. Can things be as they were, when we went wenching together after that sweet Justice's wife, your dark Mary?"

Shakespeare looked at him. "Wenching together" was not as he remembered it.

And very soon, like a lover who cannot bear a parting, Will

went to the bedchamber to where his boy was talking to the caged bird. Hal stood in the doorway, a glass in his hand, and said lightly, "So that is what you love."

"Love? Yes. That is the word at last."

"We shall escape together from our families. Soon. When you grow tired of the prattling of children." Hal turned away and left those two Shakespeares together.

\* \* \*

Shakespeare brought Hamnet down to the Theatre where we rehearsed the *Dream of Midsummer* and, if the father wanted a mug of bastard ale at the end of a dry practice, Hamnet would remind him that Mother Parker had supper ready for them, and she didn't like to be kept waiting. All of which Shakespeare took in good part. But one night, when he was sat at home, before the chill white of an empty paper, trying to write that scene of the comedy which we had to have on the morrow if we would do the play (Dick Burbage had threatened to revive *Tamburlaine the Great* if Will had not the scene ready) he longed for company and said as much to Hamnet.

"They are mistaken, boy – about the way we poets work!"

"Are they, Father?"

"Ned Alleyn, the actor in the old time, when I was first apprenticed to the craft, used to lock up the poor poet Marlowe, like a slave or a man condemned! I mind ... I mind, now, how Marlowe, in his turn, locked me in. By a stratagem. So I would do a scene for him."

Hamnet came to look at his father's paper, and was not overcome by his industry. "Father!"

"I tell you, Hamnet. And this will be of use to you if you go for a poet, which you shall with your true ear and delicate imaginings. I tell you, boy. The secret of this craft – " Shakespeare was now striding the room, whilst Hamnet protested.

"Father. You have only ten lines written!"

"It's not with paper and pens we work, nor in locked rooms neither. It's in the world outside! Look, what must I do now.

– tonight. Why, a piece of fooling for certain mechanicals. Can I do it cased and cribbed in this little dungeon, Hamnet? Never! But at the Dagger Inn! Now there is a new wench carries pots there who is as full of jokes and foolery as a waggon-load of clowns, and a bald-headed carpenter who speaks in phrases of nice pomposity – as he were Lord Chief Justice and not plain Ned the Joiner. And a mad Captain out of Flanders full of strange oaths and impossible boastings, with a tapster who can keep four bottles in the air juggling and dance you a jig like one mad of moon-fever! They are my tools, boy. They are the very stuff of my profession! Much better I study them than gaze upon this barren whiteness! You agree, Hamnet, I'm sure," he ended hopefully.

He got no word of encouragement from his son, so he went out to the bedchamber to fetch a thick cloak against the chill of a dirty night. At which Hamnet locked the chamber door on the outside, passed down the passage and into the bedroom, and, as his father went cloaked into the chamber, locked the bedroom door also, making the poet as tight a prisoner as was ever Marlowe to Alleyn. When Shakespeare discovered his plight he beat on both doors furiously.

"I'll sleep in here, father, so I won't disturb your writing," came young Hamnet's voice from the bedroom.

"What are you, boy? A poet or an actor?" Shakespeare called, enraged.

"I'm just trying to look after you, sir."

At which soft answer the poor poet sat down at his desk. Indeed, there was nothing else for him to do.

"As you say, Lord Tyrant," he said. "I'd best put off living until tomorrow."

\*  \*  \*

So was the scene written and it proved, to my thinking, the most comical, absurd and pleasing in all his comedies : it was that part in which the foolish mechanicals enact the play of *Pyramus and Thisbe*. And when we had all laughed at it, and the parts were copied, why then we all went to the Dagger with a clear conscience. Hamnet came with us and I noticed that, very privily, Dick Burbage gave the boy money, which I think can only have been for locking up his father. And then Dick had Shakespeare engaged in a long discussion about some ludicrous business to make the clowns clumsier and the moonshine more absurd, when the poet remembered him of an arranged meeting.

"Hamnet. Good boy. Run home, I pray you. Say I'll be there in five minutes." And thinking to have arranged his business he set about to explain to Burbage that his idea was wrong and that a clown will only make you laugh if his clowning still has the quality of human behaviour.

* * *

Mother Parker let her up into the chamber where she stood before the mirror and raised her veil. She was Mary Fleminge, who had left home on the pretext of taking some alms to the poor, in truth to do some charity to a poet hungry for Love's Banquet. And as she looked in the mirror she saw a small, large-eyed boy, staring at her.

"Who are you?"

"Hamnet Shakespeare, madam. Son to the Poet."

"Of course, you have his very brow. His nose too. Your father teaches me the wonders of poetry." Mary seemed to think she best try to explain her presence, the more so as the big-eyed boy sat staring at her. "Will he be back soon?" she asked him.

"*They* will be back soon." Hamnet's voice carried the threat unmistakable.

"*They?*"

"My father. And my mother."

"Your *what*?"

"My mother, madam."

At which Mistress Fleminge was up and quick to go as a doe startled from a covert, though first she did her best to hide her traces.

"Dear God! To make an engagement, and then have a

wife about him! He would scandal my reputation!" She forced a smile at Hamnet. "Boy. Sweet boy. Sweet, handsome boy. Here is a sovereign. A golden sovereign. Buy custard and all else you have a mind to. Only don't tell your mother of my visit."

Hamnet took the money. He was earning well that day, for a ten year old.

Mary tried to put some terror into the unblinking boy. "If you tell. If! I'll have a spell put on you! By a witch I know in Cheapside. A beldam crone I have in fee to me. She'll turn your blood to water!"

"Who are you, lady?" Hamnet asked her, putting away her money.

"No matter. Never mind my name. Your father called me his dark lady always. Now, promise me. You have forgot I was ever here!"

\*     \*     \*

Shakespeare had soon settled the question of the clowns business with Burbage and was at his door when he met Mistress Fleminge coming out. Their meeting was short and most unloving.

"What is it – a trap? To make a fool of me? Home to your wife now, Master Husband! I'll none of you!"

"Wife ... Wife? Who talks of a wife?" Shakespeare was bewildered.

"Your son! He told me she is with you here."

"My son?"

"Fare you well, Master Married! I'll go fish single men for company."

\*     \*     \*

"You lied to her!" For the first time in his life Shakespeare was in a rage with Hamnet.

"Only to make her go away. I didn't like her."

"Your liking her is nothing to the point. I like her! *I* ..."

"Then she is not worthy of your liking, sir." Hamnet was calm and quite decided.

"She's not?"

"Dark and stupid. And not beautiful."

"What should I do, my Lord Fastidious? Call for Helen of Troy like old Doctor Faustus?"

"Better you work at your writing, Father, than waste hours with such as she. I saw she wore fine lace on her sleeves. I hope you do not spend on her."

"What if I do?" Shakespeare was amazed. The boy made him feel to blame.

"Then you are foolish, Father."

Where had he heard that voice? Shakespeare closed his eyes, and knew immediately. "It is! It is my sour wife transformed to a boy! I swear to you, Hamnet! Living with you is a marriage. I may not go out to dinner but I ask your permission. I may not go to work but I question whether you find the play tedious. And I may not love or I face your wrath, your sulks, your silences! Listen to me. That dark lady you saw, I have spent years in the wooing and winning of. And now she's gone. Frightened off. Gone to covert! So what is left to me but to dredge the taverns and the wine shops and find such light ladies as you have left me?" At the door he gave the boy a parting shot, "Goodnight wife!" So he was gone about his pleasures, and who knows if the boy cried or no?

After a night when the wine followed the bastard ale, and the Brandy followed the Burgundy, when Susan at the Dagger gave place to Meg at the Angel and then to some person unknown about dawn in the back room of a wine tavern, with his head splitting, his eyes red, his shirt filthy, his purse light and his once-proud sentinel drooping with exhaustion, Will Shakespeare returned home to meet the sharp nosed Mother Parker emptying the slops.

"What a time to come home!"

"I am home early."

"It's near ten o'clock in the morning!"

"So it's early to be home." He thought that a brave jest,

but quit laughing when Mother Parker said, "He's gone!"

"Gone? Where has he gone?" He began to run up the stairs, suddenly afraid.

Mother Parker called up after him, "Home to his mother, let's hope. Well, it's not a life for a boy here, is it? No life at all."

# 25

## *Of How Hamnet Shakespeare*
## *Went Home To Stratford*

SHAKESPEARE WAS PLAYING Philostrate, master of the revels, but never was there such a pale and woeful face as his when we gathered in the tiring room before the play. He had paid a fellow to ride post to Stratford, but wondered how so small a child could have found his way back to his mother.

"I wonder he wasn't here before now," said Alex Cooke. "He usually waits in the tiring room."

"Hop on time always! More punctual than actors." Hemminge was ever businesslike.

"Let him be, Will. Perhaps he's found a wench of his own." Will Kempe was not much comfort, but Sam Cross told us that all boys return home, when it's time for supper.

"He will be back to you," I tried to cheer Will. "He'll not go back to his mother and silence."

"Come, Hearts," Burbage was calling, "The Playhouse is full. There are Lords on stage and Knights on the balconies and we have a play forward."

From the first line that *Dream of a Midsummer Night* laid its spell upon our audience. There was laughter and clapping, and then, as the mechanicals did their clownish play, as enacted through a chink in the wall, and as Alex Cooke, in a long tow wig and a silly female dress, lisped "I see a voice", Will Shakespeare heard a sound sweeter than all the applause he had ever had, his son laughing from a balcony. So when the play was done he ran to the place and lifted Hamnet,

whose laughter had now turned to a sore coughing, from his
fine seat.

"I looked for you at the lodgings. And you were all the
time in the Theatre. How came you in?"

"I have money. I bought a seat in the balcony. It's cold
now the play is over. I meant to ask you, sir. Whatever befell
the changeling boy?"

"Why, the King and the Queen stopped quarrelling over
him. Come." He picked up Hamnet in his arms. The boy was
shivering.

"When shall we go home?" Hamnet asked, he seemed very
tired.

"Why, now. We'll have supper. Then you shall to bed.
Tomorrow ... Why, tomorrow we shall ride out into the
country."

\*        \*        \*

I know not if Hamnet had ever been weak, truly his mother
spoke of a cough and gave him syrup for it. I know not if, on
that night he was alone, he set out to seek his father and so
took cold; but the next day they rode not out, and the day
after Shakespeare called on the good Doctor Moffett, and
was heard haranguing him on the stairs.

"What is it, man? Speak, Doctor!"

"There is a sour rheum there and an ague and perhaps a
rotten lung, but I know not. And a cholic. For sure there is a
cholic. Whatever there is it must be drawn out with a bleed-
ing and a bathing of the limbs in hot water."

"Mother Parker, set on hot water!" Shakespeare shouted,
and got a sour reply.

"This is a gentleman's lodgings, not a hospital!"

"Before God, I'll choke you, woman, if you don't bring
boiling water to my son!"

Doctor Moffett, who was, out of long practice, calm in the
face of sickness, however puzzling, continued, "And we shall
administer many simples of garlic, colocynth and coloquin-
tida. If *that* answers not ..."

"If ... ?"

"Then we bind his throat with an old stocking. And if *that* answers not ..."

"Then?" Shakespeare was quiet now.

"Then we wish your son a safe journey to where we all must go in the end." Doctor Moffett crossed himself and went out to fetch herbs and leeches. He could hear Shakespeare shouting as he left, "Never! Never! Never say it! Where's that hot water, woman?"

When he went into the bedroom Hamnet was pale on his pillow and his eyes seemed larger and more wondering than ever. Shakespeare sat on the bed and took his son's hand.

"You're tired, little poet. Only tired."

"The lady said she'd have me bewitched. Has she?"

"Bewitched! Nonsense. We'll soon have you better. Do you not trust me, boy?"

"I think, sir, she has bewitched me."

"I brought you to speak again and to ... to argue with me and to laugh. Well, then, if I can make you laugh there's no witchcraft can harm you. No, nor illness either. Trust me, boy. I am your best of doctors. Tell me, it pleased you, did it not? That short and comical *Dream of a Midsummer's Night*?"

It was a long time before Hamnet answered and then he said, "When shall I go home? To Stratford?"

\* \* \*

Hamnet went back home and was buried in a small grave in Stratford churchyard. They stood together in the rain, his mother and father, his two sisters, neighbour Hamnet Sadler and Judith. The earth fell on him and he was silent as ever, so no one can know if he would ever have made a poet.

When they came back to the cold house Anne asked her husband if he must go back to London, and he told her yes, that he must go and could not stay for dinner. There was no forgiveness in either of their voices.

When he got to his lodgings Shakespeare found Hamnet's thrush "Puck" caged in the bedroom. He went to the window, opened up the door of the cage and released the bird into the sky.

# Part Five

## "REBELLION IN HIS WAY"

*"Rebellion lay in his way and he
found it."*

Henry IV, Part 1

# 26

## Of Heroes and Hero-Worship

WHEN YOU COME to my advanced age, I promise you, it makes no great difference who governs you, your main concern being to get a piece of cheese to mumble, a bone of meat on Sunday, and to wake up in the morning still more or less alive. To which truth I make one great exception. I would rather, if God pleases, not be ruled by the Puritans, who are to the rest of our sane citizenry as snakes are to earth worms, or vinegar to a fine soft wine of Bordeaux. These canting, snivelling, neutered hypocrites have closed our theatres, flogged our actors, stopped for all eternity (unless some decent citizen do boot their backsides and put them out of office) our Great English Art of Playmaking. No doubt they will go on to forbid Nursery Rhymes, punish Roses for wearing too rich a perfume and end up by enforced lopping off of all men's codpieces as leading too directly to the sin of pleasure, while the sweet boxes of young girls will be padlocked by Order of Parliament. (This I have writ is of great danger and I would burn it, save that it is now dawn, the candle is guttered and gone out, and I have no fire left but that poor flame within me which will still boil my hatred of these same poxy Puritans.)

Now Will Shakespeare had been rebuked by Kit Marlowe for not concerning himself with the Great Drama Politic; but as that Machieval of a playmaker ended with two inches of steel cooling his brain in the sludge at Deptford, his

example served rather to deter Shakespeare from too close
an interest in the affairs of State, unless they took place some
time safely back in the bloodstained reign of the Second
Richard, or Harry Four.

I cannot be sure, indeed, how he felt on the matter of
Authority, and of Government. He made the wily Ulysses
speak of order and degree as the string which, tuned, kept
regular all the music of the spheres, yet when he was in the
mood of it Will Shakespeare could rail most powerfully
against authority, saying a dog would be obeyed in office, and
crying, "Handy Dandy, which is the Justice, which the
Thief?" Now which of these two contrary opinions he held to
most strongly I know not, but as his *Tragedy of King Lear*
must be accounted a finer play ever than his *Troilus and
Cressida* (wherein the unpleasant Ulysses voices such respectable opinions) I must hold that his attitude before the Powers
that Govern our lives was not of the most unblinking adula-
tion.

At the time I now recollect, Kit Marlowe had been long
years in the grave, and Shakespeare had forgot the salutary
lesson that Dead Shepherd's life should have taught him. He
was therefore tempted to meddle in matters Politic, and you
shall learn how near to disaster such temptation brought us
all. And the tempter herein was not Mephistopheles but the
more nobly born Robert Devereux, Earl of Essex, friend and
hero to our poet's friend, Henry Wriothesley, Earl of Southampton.

I told you how Hal knew Robin Essex when they were
both wards of old Lord Burghley, and how the little boy Hal
so worshipped the big boy Robin who could outride, out-tilt
and outdance any of the young men in that breeding ground
of fine young pacers. But Robin did all that Hal wished for
and never achieved, not only could he dance and write verses
both in the English and Latin tongues, he was sent at eighteen
as General of the Horse to the Netherlands, appointed there
by another Earl, that of Leicester, then the Queen's favourite.
Later Robin Essex replaced Leicester in that Old Virgin's
heart, and he expressed his undying love and amazement at

the Celestial Beauty of his Sovereign, though she were some thirty-three years older than he, bald but for a few whispy hairs under her scarlet wig, and the least likely body in the whole world that a young sprig of the aristocracy would like to tumble. However, no doubt his frequent protestations of love caused her old heart to flutter most delightfully, and they did him no harm, bringing him all sorts of riches and honours, the monopoly of sweet wines and the joint command, with Lord Howard of Effingham, of the attack on the Spanish Harbour of Cadiz, when Essex threw his hat in the sea, sacked the town, but only brought home a tiny part of the gold and jewels there taken, allowing most of the booty to be foisted by the sailors. Truly Robin Essex, though ever a man for a fine gesture, was not the most practical of persons.

The Queen, who cared as much for grasping coin as she did for hanging on to life, was not much pleased by this negligence: but by his famous victory Robin Essex became a Great Hero to all the people, who saw him ever in glittering armour, yelling defiance at England's Popish, Spanish, conniving and plotting enemies, standing upon the poop of some English ship and defiantly throwing his hat into the sea. The people loved him and for his friend young Hal, weary of marriage and an uneventful life, he was ever the Hero *non pareil*

Such love, of course, brings enemies. That crookback son of old Burghley, Robert Cecil, whom Hal and Robin had teased in their childhood days, putting frogs in his bed sheets and smearing the stair with butter when he came down for prayers so he near broke his neck, that same Robert Cecil was, by dint of tireless working and the supreme cunning of his brain, Master Secretary Cecil and, perhaps remembering his humiliations at the hands of young Essex, and also being envious of so straight a body and so fine a head, set about plots to displace Essex from the Queen's favour. His most successful move was to help Essex to the High Office of General in Ireland, for the purpose of suppressing the Irish Rebels. Essex received this post with some delight, but it was to prove his sentence of death. For as no one has ever

truly succeeded in the suppression of the Irish Rebels, his
task was, from the outset, doomed to failure.

The trouble was that the Irish Rebels would not stand
still long enough to be suppressed. They'd slide in and out of
their cursed bogs like the starved ghosts of water spaniels:
and would not ride up and do battle, or be killed like gentlemen. Hal was taken to Ireland and given a high command,
and proved a fine horseman as he was a brave soldier, and a
more sensible captain even than his Hero, the Lord General.
For Essex was a miserable dog in Ireland, his fine armour
rusted in the mist, his men took bog-ague or leaked away
and married Irish colleens, he could never meet the enemy
in battle and he had little to do in the evenings except confer
on his close friends knighthoods for deeds of chivalry that
they had no opportunity to perform. Worst of all, he had
intelligences from England that Robert Cecil was making
himself Master Secretary Indispensable to the Queen and
was dropping certain hints about the possible danger to Her
Majesty of the People's Hero being at the head of a mighty
army but a day's sail across the Irish Sea.

So Robin Essex decided he must come home which his
orders forbade him to do, without the express leave of the
Queen in Council. All the same, he met the rebel leader
Tyrone in the mist, on a green bridge over a slimy stream,
and, finding the Erse Leader a kind of poetic, eloquent and
reassuring down-at-heel gentleman, struck not swords but
terms of peace with him, not knowing that peace terms in
Ireland are but as candles left out in a December snow, not
like to last till morning. That done he took a few of his bolder
and more determined captains, Hal the Hero Worshipper and
Christopher St. Lawrence, Charles Danvers, Gilly Merrick
and that Sir Christopher Blount who at moments of excitement was want to cry "Saw, saw, saw, tray, tray, tray", as
though he were following hounds on his bony mare through
the wet woods of his home county.

This muddy, desperate cavalcade clattered into the Royal
Palace at Nonesuch one morning and Robin Essex, half
Ireland on his boots, dirt on his face and his sword at his side,

burst into his Queen's bedchamber as she sat at her dressing table, without her wig, her old head bald and her papery face naked of those paints and powders with which she was about to draw on it a strange caricature of youth. When told of this outrage Robert Cecil gave a small, cold smile and bade his servants do nothing. Given enough rope, he knew, the Earl of Essex would hang no one but himself, unless it were his foolish hero-worshippers.

It is not for me, old Jack Rice, though I saw the Queen when we did the play for her, to speculate what went on in the Sovereign's bedchamber (though if speculation be in order I had rather dream of the happenings in the bed-chamber of that sweet sprauncy young wife of Cheapside who came to Church on Sunday and who, even as I handed her a prayer book, I undressed in my mind's eye). Belike, the Queen was much alarmed and then, when she heard of the Peace with Tyrone very angry, and finally, controlling her fear and her anger, and that last tickle of love when she saw her muddy Earl kneel before her and promise adoration till the soul did leave his prison body, she did command him to take and wash his prison body and, having changed his shirt and put on clean breeches, to await her word in the Great Hall at Nonesuch.

When, cleaned and perfumed as for the lists of love, Robin Essex went in to the Great Hall, he found precious few courtiers, a great many armed Halberdiers, and his friends sent home already. Then, they say, came Lord Keeper Egerton to him with a message from his Sovereign. But there was no word of love, only that the Earl was placed under arrest and must straight to Essex House, not to stir from thence without leave of the Privy Council. All this was observed by Robert Cecil from his bird's nest of a balcony looking over the Great Hall and, though he did not laugh out loud as Robin Essex did when they buttered the stairway, no doubt he was smiling unusually.

# 27

## *Of An Unhappy Family*

THE PEOPLE WERE discontented, their great hero, the Eagle Essex, was caged, and furthermore the weather was appalling, and furthermore our family of actors was all ajangle with quarrels, jealousies and discontent, and furthermore business was extremely poor, we lacked feet on the ground and buttocks on the seats. Our ills may be itemised.

*Item One*   Since his *Dream of Midsummer* ended in the burial of his young rascal, a sort of melancholy hung about Will Shakespeare. Indeed, when he wrote a comedy it was of a very sad and wistful sort, a kind of autumn piece that was full of sad sighs at departing youth and coming mists. Now such a play comical did catch, as I think, all the sadness that lies in the merriest jest: but it pleased not the groundlings who like an unthinking laugh from the guts and a guffaw to clear the chest before they pass on to dinner.

*Item Two*   Will Kempe the dancing clown and King of Jollity fitted not so well into this season of melancholy. Shakespeare found us one Robert Armin, who, with a whey face and a sweet-sad voice was a clown *non pareil* to break your heart over. As you may well think, this pleased not Will Kempe who woke every day in a vile ill mood, swore at everyone and tried to drown his sorrows deep in many gallons of bastard ale.

*Item Three*   Augustine Phillips, who once did play older women, having grown so burly he now did undertake second heroes (Hotspur, Mercutio and the like), we engaged one Mark Coombe to discharge older ladies. This actor was of an exceeding nervous disposition, for ever dropping his properties, missing his cues and tripping on his entrances. He skulked in a corner of the tiring room and would speak to no one, and his presence but added to the irritation of us all.

So I come to the time when I, as the lovely Viola, fell down into the grave trap in full view of the audience.

We played that comical-sad piece *What you Will* or *Twelfth Night* as it was called afterwards (that it was played on Twelfth Night in Middle Temple Hall). As I came to the Theatre I had seen a black coated fellow with an Irish sing-song voice speak to some who might have bought places, and as he spoke I saw them turn away. I heard later that he told them, quite falsely, that there was to be no play that afternoon as Will Kempe was dead drunk (trust he was dead drunk, but that never stopped him playing). So the audience was thin, Armin sang sweetly sad as Feste the Jester, Kempe vowed in the tiring room that our new clown had as many laughs in him as a baby's open grave and on the stage sat Hal Southampton and those saucy knights Danvers, St. Lawrence, Merrick and Blount, who chattered loudly of their hero's martyrdom and house arrest and hardly heard the play.

Which was their misfortune. There was I once more, the beautiful Jack Rice, a boy playing a girl who plays a boy, wooing Dick Burbage as the Duke Orsino.

> "My father had a daughter loved a man
>    As it might be perhaps, were I a woman
>    I should your Lordship."

I looked at Dick and loved him to despair, though in life there had never been a touch or a kiss between us.

> "What's her history?"

"We'll rescue Robin. And all the town shall rise to us!"

swore Sir Charles Blount, loudly enough to interrupt the
scene.

And Hal had the grace to whisper, "Hush and attend the
play."

"'And what's her history?'" said Dick-Orsino.

God's death, how I remember the lines, too sad for a
comedy, too beautiful almost for speaking in a theatre.

> "A blank, my Lord. She never told her love
>     But let concealment like a worm i' the bud
>     Feed on her damask cheek: she pined in thought
>     And with a green and yellow melancholy
>     She sat like Patience on a monument
>     Smiling at grief ..."

At which I took one more step towards Dick, there was a
sudden noise of wood rending, the ground gave under me,
I fell through the grave trap and gave the audience their
best laugh of the play.

As I went down I swear I saw that dark man I had heard
speak in an Erse tone of voice among the groundlings smiling.

Later, when my cuts were bandaged and my bruises colour-
ing nicely, we all gathered round the grave trap and Sam
Crosse showed us where the joist under the door was near
sawn through. Hal had loitered after the play and was standing with us, where he could see us also.

"Treachery!" Alex Cooke had no doubt about it.

"Dear heart! You have played too many histories." Burbage
ever believed the best of people.

"Use your brains," Will Kempe belched out at Dick. "If
they be not all addled with food and finery. A man turns
away our customers, a man saws the grave trap near in two
so we may break legs – pray God they were not mine else
you had lost the best caperer in England!"

"You can spare a leg, Will Kempe," I told him. "Sure, you
see each one double!"

"Who would go to such pains to stop a play?" Even
Shakespeare looked puzzled.

"We have enemies. Those that hate us and wish us evil!" Alex Cooke was sure of it. As he said this Hal moved among us, strong, gentle and reassuring, friend to the Great Earl of Essex, the people's Hero.

"The Child Actors of St. Paul's are jealous of us." Will Kempe was sure of it. "This is their work."

"You breed enemies, my friends. With your great talents. Malice and jealousy will soon marry and give birth to violence. You need a strong power to protect you."

"Your power, Hal?" Shakespeare smiled, doubtful.

"A greater power than mine. One who may command armies and soon will command ... Well, 'tis best you know not what he may command."

"One who may command armies! That would be a General!" Sam Crosse was breathless with awe.

"We need a cannon against those bloodthirsty child actors of St. Paul's." Will Kempe could not forget the little horribles.

But Hal had an arm about my shoulder, and one round Dick Burbage to comfort us all. "Come. Let me teach you how you may come secretly to the great Earl of Essex. For sure, he will guard your liberties. Even to the death!"

# 28

## *Of How The Actors Brought Music To The Earl*

THERE WERE SIX of us of the party, Hal, Will Shakespeare, Will Kempe, Jack Rice and Robert Armin. At the last moment that trembling custard Mark Coombe asked if he might come. We took him as he had a voice that sang in tune, though with no great strength, and it was so rare that he plucked up courage to ask anything that we could not refuse him when he begged to come with us. We put on masks and big hats, long black cloaks for a disguise, and we took with us lutes, viols and a tabor and all set out to Essex House.

This none too uncomfortable prison was guarded by the Queen's Halberdiers, but the Captain of Helberds, either from idleness or corruption, was admitting all such as said they came with victuals, wine, small beer or other necessities for his Lordship's table, and it seemed that a whole gang of roughs and desperadoes was being let in to the courtyard of Essex House in the pretence that they were butchers, bakers, or fishmongers. "The Earl's meat!" they would cry. "The Earl's barrel of oysters", even "The Earl's carving knives", and I wondered how many swords and daggers went in under that general description. "The Earl's music!" cried Hal in a high voice from behind his mask. And we were let pass through.

So we came into a high chamber in which was burning a great fire; over it a picture of Her Virgin Majesty looked down glassy eyed on our proceedings. In front of it sat Lord Robert Devereux, Earl of Essex, in a shirt, scarlet

breeches and stockings with a book in his hand. As we came
in and did our bows to him he began to say verses, looking
into the fire as if he thought himself to be alone. I had never
seen the Earl of Essex before and truly he was of a great
magnificence with his long nose well shaped, his eye deep
and lustrous, his lip full red and fixed in a wry smile, his hair
fair and his beard auburn.

"For God's sake let us sit upon the ground," he intoned,
"And tell sad stories of the death of Kings; How some have
been deposed ..." On that word 'deposed' he laid particular
stress. "... All murdered, for within the hollow crown, That
rounds the mortal temples of a King, Keeps death his Court,
And at the last, and with a little pin ..." Here the Earl drew
his dagger and fingered the point, "... Bores through his
castle walls and farewell King."

Now the Earl of Essex had quite botched the lines Shakespeare wrote for the Second Richard, forgetting many of
them and patching others together, but he sounded as he
said them much like an actor. Sure he was playing a role in
the theatre of his ambitions; but he played it worse than an
actor would, and, like no real actor I have ever known when
he recited it caused a strange embarrassment.

"Talk not of sadness and death." Hal, still masked, stepped
forward and bowed. "We have come to divert you with
music."

So Essex bade his pages bring us wine. Will Kempe danced
and capered and Armin sang with sweet, sad certainty,

> "What is love, 'tis not hereafter
> Present mirth hath present laughter
> What's to come is still unsure ..."

As Armin sang Essex drew Hal aside and we all heard him
say, "Hal, I am offered my place back by the Queen if I will
but kneel to Her Privy Council and confess my faults."

"Will the Queen keep her bargain?" Hal asked him. And the
answer came so cold and full of hate none of us could forget it.

"I'll trust her no longer," Essex swore. "Her ways are as
crooked as her carcass."

Armin sang on hurriedly,

> "In delay there lies no plenty
>     So come and kiss me sweet and twenty
>     Youth's a stuff will not endure . . ."

"Sweet words and a good catch nobly sung," said the Earl, and bade his page pass amongst us with more wine. And then, as we all unmasked to drink, I saw the Earl go, most respectfully, to Will Shakespeare.

"Master Shakespeare, truly you are the only man in this Kingdom whose strength I envy," said Essex, which so astonished the poet that he said,

"My Lord, we have but the strength of shadows."

"You do yourself wrong! You may work more good with a line of verse, a word even, than I may do with all the swords and spears come out of Ireland. And I tell you, we are both actors, you and I." What was this? The Great Robert Devereux, Earl of Essex, the Lord General, sworn of the Privy Council, putting himself on the level of a poor player.

"You have the world's stage, my Lord. I am confined to a little theatre and a dwindling audience." For the first time I thought Will Shakespeare sounded envious.

"But from that very theatre may come words that will save England from her enemies and make you a power in the land," Essex told him, but Shakespeare still seemed not to understand.

"A power, my Lord?"

"I have heard you have the first sign of power – enemies!"

Now this was clear to us. This was what we had come for, his Lordship's help against our enemies.

"True. We have enemies that did turn away our audience," said Kempe.

"And sawed the grave trap near in two," Armin told him.

"Poor young Jack Rice, him that does play the petticoat parts, near broke his ankles," Coombe took the courage to say, flutingly.

"And you can't play petticoats in crutches," I told them.

"You have strong enemies. Why, so have I. And we'll defeat them both! Look, I have twenty men-at-arms below who'll guard your theatre." At which the Earl of Essex sent word by a page to tell the Captain of his Roughs and Rowdies to keep a special eye on us. Then he came near to Shakespeare, and Hal came up on his other side, so there was the poet, set between two Earls, and the one in scarlet tempted him.

"I await a call to a great place in this Kingdom," said Essex. "And when it comes, why, you shall be beside me. Your words and our deeds, sir. What may not the three of us gain together?"

So he looked at Hal, who also tempted. "True, you shall be first in our councils, Will!"

"I am but a poet." Now Shakespeare seemed not quite sure that was all he could be.

"And we need a poet! We have Captains enough. Hal tells me you are his friend always."

"Yes." Apart from a small rift over a dark lady.

"And a friend to our just cause?"

"I would wish your Lordship strong to defeat our enemies." That was the poet, diplomatic.

"Then grant me one favour only! Do but let your players enact the Tragedy of the Second King Richard, his most deserved Deposition, wherein a Prince falls by false and treacherous advice. And England is saved by a new power! What, are you afraid? I'll not believe him who wrote that scene feared anything."

"What can a play do?"

"Do? Why, it can bring you out of your little stage into the world. You'll not be a poet merely but the equal of all the peers in council!"

Shakespeare had writ the play of the Second Richard some five years before. And why were the two Earls so fond of it? Not for its sad, echoing poetry, not for the strange sight of a King sinking exquisitely in a sea of words, but because that play showed a monarch deposed by a great general – and if the groundlings could see it happen once, might they not

think it could be done again? "No Sovereign is immortal, nor
does the divine will keep her bum glued to the chair of
State." This was the lesson Essex hoped the world might learn
in the Theatre were the Second Richard to be played again.

And Will Shakespeare heard all this. I think he understood
most of it, and he was tempted. To be of Essex's council when
Essex ruled! Then he would be, indeed, God's playmaker:
to say how men must act on the stage of life itself, to bring
them on at a line, and, when they had done their use, speed
them towards their exits. So he looked at us, the actors, and
said quietly, "The Tragedy of the Second Richard! What say
you, can we do that play again?"

"Do so and we are brothers until death!" Essex assured us
all.

"We cannot play for nothing," Will Kempe was bold to say.

"For my Lord's fancy!" Hal seemed to think we should be
flattered.

"With respect, we cannot live on my Lord's fancy."

"Would forty shillings buy your house out, actor?"

"Aye, and give us a gallon of ale to drink his Lordship's
health."

"God bless the Earl of Essex! But we are rusty with the
words, and Burbage . . . poor Burbage will no longer fit the
costume."

"Tush, man! I have some old suits of clothing. More
than one man's back may wear." It was true he gave Augustine
Phillips a suit of his own scarlet velvets to enact the deposer
Bolingbroke. "I have that scene almost by heart when the
weak King Richard must yield up the crown."

"The deposition!" Hal rolled the word round his tongue
like a mouthful of fine wine.

When we left I saw a dark face in a doorway and heard
the singing of an Irish voice. It was that same servant who
had been turning folk from our Theatre. So was it the
conniving Earl that persecuted us that we might fly to him
for help? Not wishing to alarm the other actors I kept such
thoughts to myself, and the thoughts in their turn kept me
from my sleep.

# 29

## *Of How We Played To A Full House, And The Earl To No Audience*

HERCULES, WHO WAS then about Essex House with his master Southampton, told me that the roughs and bully boys ever increased in the courtyard, like maggots in a bad cheese. On that cold February Saturday a messenger came from the Queen requiring the Earl to attend the Council. Mud was thrown over the messenger's clothes, and word was sent back that the noble rebel would not stir. But now it was Hal's opinion that the Queen had decided to lay hold of Essex in stricter arrest and he must move quickly or Cecil would have him silenced for ever.

So that afternoon, it is now clear for no good purpose of playing but to show the brute people that Kings be not immortal nor thrones quite out of the reach of rebels, we played the Second Richard, I being petticoated as that sad Monarch's French Queen. And never has it been worse for actors to play to a full house than it was for us that Saturday afternoon in our fine new Theatre, that Great Globe we had built to our own designings on Bankside in order, as I now think, not to show the tears or laughter in man's life, but to play politics for an Ambitious Earl.

The Theatre filled early, but whereas I suspected before men were turned away, now they were near driven in at dagger point by some of those very roughs and bawcocks that had been frequenting Essex House. So there was soon not a place to squeeze the thinnest buttocks in the balconies, and the ground was packed to bursting. And the Audience sat there glum and silent, caring not at all for Burbage's poetic grief as Richard, nor for my beauty, till we came to the great Deposition Scene where the King is forced to give up his crown in Westminster Hall to the Usurping Bolingbroke, who has the strong claim of an army of lances and a city full of murderous apprentices to enforce his claim.

"To do what service am I sent for hither?" Wearily Burbage looked round at the faces of our audience which would indeed have frightened a far braver King than Richard Two.

"To do that office of thine own good will
    Which tired majesty did make thee offer."

so said Sam Crosse as the Duke of York,

"The resignation of thy state and crown!"

At which the Roughs cheered and shouted and the citizens, cued by the Roughs or pricked by their daggers, yelled their approval. And when we came to the line, "May deem that you are worthily deposed" there was such a shouting and yelling and a throwing up of hats that a small fat citizen in the front row of the groundlings, seeking to please the Roughs about him, shouted himself into such a fit that he vomited up his dinner. After the deposition they all fell sullen again, and half of them didn't stay for the murder at the end.

On the Sunday morning, hearing of the Great Congregation of the dangerous and undesirable, no lesser dignitaries than the Lord Keeper Egerton and Lord Bracton, the Lord Chief Justice of England, went down to Essex House (I am in debt to old Hercules the tavern-keeper for these following recollections of what he saw in his childhood as a page). After being admitted through the Great Gate they were met by my Lord Southampton, who bowed with great courtesy and asked their pleasure.

"Her Majesty's Privy Council, having heard of strange gatherings and unpermitted visitors with ..." Lord Keeper Egerton looked about him, "base fellows congregating, sends to the Earl of Essex for his immediate presence before them."

At this the Roughs murmured, but Hal silenced them

holding up his hand. "What would you with my Lord?"

"He is to come to Council to explain this disobedience," said the Lord Chief Justice.

"He will come to Council in his own good time, my Lord Chief Justice. Meanwhile he bids you stay to dinner!"

At which Hal dropped his hand, the Roughs and Saucy Knights set upon the two old men and they were constrained in a small antechamber and made to stay whether they liked it or not: none of which proceedings helped the Earl much at the later trial before my Lord Chief Justice.

Matters had clearly gone too far now to be put back and the Earl resolved to go out and raise the City of London to the Essex cause. Hal ran up a flight of stairs in the Great Courtyard and announced the entrance of the Hero.

"The time has come, my friends!" Cheers, shouts and spits from the Roughs. "Time for my Lord Essex to walk forth and meet his Glory and his people's love. An end to Tyrants! An end to traitors! An end to Spain-loving Cecils in the Council Chambers. See where he comes down now!"

At which Sir Charles Blount uttered his weird and wonderful hunting cry. "An Essex! An Essex! An Essex! Saw! Saw! Saw! Tray! Tray! Tray!"

Entered then the Hero at the head of the stairs and spoke in that actor's voice which carried indeed far less conviction than Dick Burbage would have, giving the roust of the speech before Agincourt, as an invitation to death.

"But yesterday," said Essex, 'in the Theatre across the water certain actors played out a noble tragedy. The deposition of King Richard! A weak monarch, my masters. Rightly toppled for the peace of England and the good of her common people!" They all cheered at this, there was a good deal of bastard ale passing, said Hercules, and no doubt they would have cheered at anything. "Now we also play our parts, on this great stage of history! Let us dispatch them well and earn from all free spirits a thunder of applause, and, for ourselves, fame that shall make us deathless! Remember uncrowned Richard! Monarchs are mortal – Kings may be deposed!"

So they all pressed into the street. Hercules heard one ask nervously if the Queen should really be deposed, whereat Sir Charles Blount screeched, "Hanged first. Deposed after. Saw! Saw! Saw! Tray! Tray! Tray! An Essex! An Essex!"

They entered the City by Lud Gate, but the preachers that morning had been sent word by Cecil and all had been warned in Church not to go to the Earl, but to shut their doors fast against Treason. Now Treason be a word far more terrible than "Plague", for a man may die quietly of Lord Fever without the need of his guts being dragged out of him in public and burned before his living eyes. So it must be said, in short, Lord Essex's play pleased not: none came to see him, indeed as he walked towards St. Paul's Churchyard many of his bully boys drifted away from him, even the little page Hercules ran and hid behind a tombstone, having lost his taste for politics. In vain did Lord Essex cry that the Cecils were out to murder him, or that the throne of England was to be sold to the Spanish Infanta; when the leaders came to St. Paul's they were of a small company and they looked round at silent, blind and shuttered houses.

"They will come out for us. The citizens will come out for us!" Hal shouted, as if to persuade himself.

"Saw! Saw! Saw! Tray! Tray! Tray! An Essex! An Essex!" Sir Charles Blount was now hoarser than ever in his screeching. He had some effect, one door that had been ajar slammed shut.

"Quiet that raven croaking! You'd frighten their dogs!" Hal called out loud, "Open your doors, citizens. The Earl of Essex is come to shake off tyranny. Open ... your doors! For the love of England and of Essex!"

It was then they heard the sound of drums in the dark alleys round them.

"Drums!" cried Blount hopefully.

"Their 'Prentice bands! The 'Prentices are out for us!" shouted Sir Gilly Merrick.

Robin Essex smiled for the first time as he called, "This way, my bully boys! This way each brave lad who would crack a skull for England! This way!" His voice faded and the sweat ran down his face, even on that cold day, as those drummers came out of the alleys, not Rebellious Boys, but Halberdiers, well armed and skilled in the service of the Queen. Battle was joined, some sort of battle, but by nightfall it was over. Never had a play so short a time in performance, or come more tardy off as that Comical Tragedy of the Great Essex Rebellion.

But the last Act was still to come. Essex and Southampton were tried before their Peers, and Hercules was there to keep his master in a clean shirt on such an impressive occasion. There were two prosecutors, one Coke who near lost his case by railing at the Earls and the other, deadly as a serpent, was that Francis Bacon whom Essex had worked ceaselessly to raise to power and position; but who could no more have stayed loyal to a friend than he could have walked on water. The end of this final Act was so well known to everyone that their Lordships took time off to swill beer and munch biscuits before proceeding to the final verdict. Then the head of a halberd was turned towards those accused to signify "guilty" of treason.

Then did Lord Bracton pass sentence in the common form for traitors, which I have heard done in Westminster Hall, and is fine and impressive language so long as it is directed firmly at some other unfortunate. Were I to hear it said to me I think I should scarce survive the passing of it, and there would be small need for other torments to lift me into the grave.

"For the foul and manifold treasons proved against you, the sentence of this Court is that you both shall be led to whence you came, from thence to be drawn on a hurdle through the midst of the City to the Place of Execution, there to be hanged by the neck and taken down alive – your bodies to be opened and your bowels taken out and burned before your faces : your heads and quarters to be disposed of on the gates of the City. And so God have mercy on your souls."

Hercules was standing near his master, and at this he swears he heard Hal whisper to his Hero, "So, Robin, we shall make brave gate posts."

# 30

## *Of Certain Questions
Asked of the Actors*

THE FIRST ACTOR to disappear was that timid fellow Mark
Coombe. I saw a tall Man in Leather Clothes who asked
about for him, and then one day Coombe answered not to his
call and was gone from us.

Then I passed a small crowd there was gathered round
Will Kempe who was dancing with a pipe fixed in his mouth,
beating a small drum and executing a nimble burgomask like
one who is trying to see if life can offer him other employment
than that at the seemingly doomed Globe Theatre. As he
danced I saw that same Man in Leather, followed by two
Halberdiers fully armed, push their way through the crowd
and take him, still fluting and drumming, into strict custody.
At this sight did I, the young Jack Rice, piss my breeches for
fear and from then on was in a tremble every time I heard a
knock on the door lest it was a Man in Leather Garments.
Fearful of loneliness I spent much time huddled in a corner of
Will's room in the tower of the Globe, which he let me do
whilst he was writing late, so that I spoke not, nor made too
great a sound munching my apple.

One night when Will Shakespeare seemed to be working
as though he might not live to the end of the week (which
seemed to me a reasonable fear in the circumstances) Burbage
came to him, much distressed.

"What, is our Theatre cursed?" Burbage asked. "Mark
Coombe is gone these two days and now Will Kempe is not

to be found. Soon we shall not have an actor answer to his cue."

"What have I done?" Shakespeare stood and threw down his pen.

"I know not. What have you?" Burbage asked him.

"I have grown weary of this Theatre, I wanted more."

"What more?"

"What *he* promised. To go with him and see my words play their part in his great affairs."

"Lord Essex?" Burbage was not quick in understanding the world outside the Theatre, perhaps because he doubted its existence.

"We played our Richard for him; I fear we all still may answer for it." I feared so too, and sat munching quietly on my apple as Shakespeare burst out, suddenly angry, "God, it was but a play. Not a speech in Council or a battle."

"Poor foolish Earl, he'll have no need of plays where he is going, nor will your friend either." Burbage was smiling.

"My friend?"

"Hal the Horse-Thief, Hal the High and Mighty. Well, Hal is for Heaven. What, are you locked away from the world in here? You know not he is to die?"

I'm sure Will Shakespeare knew it but he had not yet told himself. Now Burbage told him his head sunk in his hands and when he looked up at us he seemed older, paler, as if some of the life were gone out of him. "They had not told me and I was afraid to ask. Hal, Hal, my poor rascal!"

Not to watch another's tears Burbage moved away from Will to the window and looked out. And there he saw something which led him to call Will Shakespeare to him. I stood up also and we three looked down on the bare stage, lit only by moonlight. There was a man crouched by the grave trap which was open, a black and gaping hole.

"Our enemy!" Burbage whispered. It was that old woman of an actor, Mark Coombe.

* * *

Whilst we were watching the timorous Coombe do his private and mysterious business at the grave trap, Will Kempe was in a room somewhere near about Westminster Hall to which he had been taken with his pipe and tabor by the Halberdiers. A big, ginger-headed man, whom he heard others call Master Bull, was questioning him whilst somewhere in the shadows sat a pale person with a crooked back, who, I must think, was none other than Master Secretary Cecil.

Many years later I shared a mug of bastard ale with Will Kempe. The old clown had long parted our company but he gave me this account of his questioning. No doubt he exaggerated his calm on that occasion, but I do believe that Her Majesty's Council got nothing from Kempe; his nature being such that he could play nothing but the Fool.

Master Bull was reading a paper, and when he spoke his voice was deep and gravelly. "You are from the Globe Theatre?"

"Yes, sir."

"A new playhouse built by the actors. Fine dung for the seeds of revolution! You played there an old ranting piece which showed the deposing of a lawful monarch. As the traitors marched into the city ... so the actors voiced their treacherous thoughts. To gaping groundlings!"

"A damned dull piece, too. I was against it. I had nothing in it but the gardener."

"We know of your knavery. You may as well confirm it." Bull looked down at the paper again. "Your name is William Kempe? Plays the fool and dances a little."

At this Kempe was outraged. "A little! You speak, sir, to the master-dancer of England. The Lord of the Burgomask. The very nine days' wonder who could dance you from London to Norwich, and may have to if things don't improve at the Theatre."

"So things go badly at the Theatre?" Bull seemed pleased.

"Worse than badly. There be plots."

"Did you say plots?"

"Devilish plots. Fiendish plots. Plots to make a Machiavelli blush and a Beelzebub tremble."

"We shall know the nature of these plots!" Bull's voice threatened but Kempe seemed not at all perturbed.

"You shall!"

"The exact nature. Do you hesitate?"

"Not at all."

"And if you will not divulge ... we have a sight to show you. Certain instruments ..."

"Lute? Recorders?" At least Kempe said he said that.

"You would be merry! Instruments, I say, on which you may stretch your bones."

"That won't be necessary," Kempe assured him hastily.

"Tell us!"

"I'm trying to!"

"Well?"

"Well, it's a foul stratagem to take my jokes from me and my dances, and give them all to a milk-faced girl-voiced fishbone of a starveling actor name of Robert Armin."

"Is that the plot, man, you were speaking of?" Furious, Bull pounded the table with a great red fist.

"Why? Can you think of a worse one?"

"Let him go. The man is but a fool." In a weary voice from the shadows Master Secretary Cecil spoke.

"You speak the truth, sir. The finest fool in England!" Kempe told him proudly.

*　　*　　*

They let Will Kempe go without harm, but Mark Coombe had not been so fortunate, as we found out when we actors, suspicious of his midnight doings by the grave trap, stood about his bed in the tiring room where he lay looking extremely sickly. His hand was clutched beneath his pillow.

"Leave me in peace, masters," Coombe whined, "for to be sure, I'm dying."

"What did you by the grave?" Burbage asked.

And I added, "Would you break our legs once more – and let the groundlings mock us?"

"I keep something hidden there," Coombe confessed.

"Something?" We moved nearer to his bed, surrounding him so he might not escape.

"Not much savings," Coombe told us. "An actor cannot make much savings. But I have no wife."

"Sure. You play older women," Sam Crosse reminded him.

"So I have made some little savings. There's some gold here. Just a few pieces of gold." At which Mark Coombe pulled out from under his pillow that which he was clutching so tightly, a paper and a bag of money.

"That you were paid for treachery!" was Condell's opinion.

"No, truly. I told them nothing. They took me to a room where a big man with ginger hair questioned me of how we came to play that Second Richard."

"That play is back to curse us," Burbage sighed.

"I said, we all decided. We actors. I told him nothing. Nothing of our visit to the Earl."

"Do you say true?" Shakespeare looked at him, frowning.

"I told him I did discharge older women and he called me Mistress Coombe and said he had an instrument would make me speak to him." Coombe seemed then in such pain and so weak he could not continue.

"They took me below and stretched me. They stretched my bones. But I told them nothing! Nothing!"

We actors looked at each other. Could this Coombe have so much courage?

"Dick Burbage!" Coombe's voice was now very faint and he could scarce hand him the paper. "It's not a lawyer's will. But an actor's will. The will of a player of the minor roles. Nurses and landladies." At which Coombe sank back on his pillow, pale as the paper Burbage now read out to us.

"All my gold and savings contained in this bag I leave ... to the actors of the Globe, to be shared equally, as I have no other family. Signed this day, by me, Mark Coombe, player."

"Best I could do, not being a learned lawyer. Will. Will Shakespeare."

Shakespeare knelt beside Coombe, and had to listen hard to catch the last words that came from him. "Yes, Mark?"

"The Council ... The Queen's Council. They have killed

me with their questioning. But I told them nothing. Do you hear? They got nothing of me."

Then Coombe lay still and Shakespeare rose from the bedside, saying bitterly, "But a play! How many must die for it?"

\* \* \*

Dick Burbage, a sweat-rag about his head, was practising at the foils for a new play Tragical of Will Shakespeare's and the rest of us were about the Theatre, some copying parts (such of us as could write well) some mending properties, some painting and mending the balconies of our new Theatre which had fallen out of repair in a bad season, when they carried Coombe's coffin out of the tiring room. Will Kempe was back with us. At that time he had told us not where he had gone and we all thought he had lain drunk in some ale house two days, and returned with his temper not wholly improved. He was drinking bastard ale as the coffin passed and Dick Burbage quit fencing and cried, "Stand, dear Hearts. Stand!"

All stood except Will Kempe. Hemminge crossed himself, "He was a brave man, was Mark Coombe."

"Brave?" Kempe sank his mug and went to the barrel to draw himself another. "He was weak as water. To die of questioning by the Privy Council!" He refreshed himself. "They questioned me and I cared not a fig for their questioning!"

There was a silence and we all looked fearfully at Kempe. We had not yet heard of his visit to the Questioners.

"You were brought to the Council?" Shakespeare asked.

"Into the very presence of Master Secretary Cecil!" Will Kempe was proud of it.

"What did you tell them?" Armin sounded frightened.

"Tell them? Why, that we had a sad fellow named Robert Armin that sang like a chained mongrel howling for a bone, and we were losing customers!" He drained one mug and poured another.

"What did they do to you?" Armin asked.

"Why, they understood me! 'A great fool such as you,' they said, 'to have to play with such a ninny. It's an outrage!' They let me go."

There was a silence, we were all troubled. Shakespeare, it was, asked him, "They racked you not, nor whipped you?"

"You sound disappointed!"

"So, you satisfied them! You told them how we visited the rebel Earl." Armin made the accusation, but we all agreed with it. How else had Kempe escaped so easily?

"I told them nothing."

"I believe you told them all." Armin had no doubt.

Kempe looked around at us and then burst out in anger, "Who calls me traitor? Who calls me that?"

None of us answered him. We all had our thoughts, mine was of that terrible sentence of treason: my stomach felt loose and there was a tightening about my neck.

"So that's it." Kempe rounded on us. "I am a traitor, am I? Good. Then I'll take my leave of you. I can make oceans of sovereigns, fluting and capering down the lanes of England, whilst you all starve, listening to his doleful dirges." He went to get his drum and fife and also his bundle. When he came back from the tiring room he shouted at us again, "I am no traitor. I am a nine days' wonder at the dance. I shall dance to Norwich and so prove it to the world!"

Kempe began to leave the Theatre, Hemminge wanted to prevent him, but Shakespeare said, "Let him go."

"But he told them all," Armin protested.

"What's done is done. Let him go, dancing."

So Will Kempe started to beat his drum, blew a little whistling tune on his fife, and danced out of the Theatre for ever. Our family was breaking apart. Truly it was a bad season with us.

Two days later I was watching the bear-bait when I saw the Man in Leather pushing his way through the press of people towards me. I closed my eyes and awaited his hand on my shoulder but he turned away, and I saw him lead away another, our sad clown Robert Armin.

# 31

## Of How Shakespeare Met a Great Power And Was Taught A Lesson In The Art Of Politics

ARMIN WAS NOT gone more than a day when I was in the tiring room and I heard a voice from the stage, singing truly,

> "Come away. Come away, death,
> And in sad Cyprus let me be laid,
> Fly away, fly away breath
> I am slain by a fair cruel maid."

I went on to the stage. Armin was alone, practising his singing to the lute.

> "My shroud of white, stuck o'er with yew
> O prepare it!
> My part of death, no one so true
> Did share it."

I walked towards him. He looked up at me. I said, "You're back."

"Yes."

"They racked not you, neither?"

"The man there said he loved my singing. So he asked no questions." He would not look at me but struck again at his lute. I knew then he had told them all.

The next morning the Man in Leather and two Halberdiers fully armed came to take away Will Shakespeare.

They took our playmaker to the Palace of Nonesuch, where all our troubles began with the Earl of Essex interrupting, so rudely and without invitation, Her Majesty's dressing. They put him, closely watched, in a guard room and then a steward came and took him to an antechamber and left him there waiting, attended only by a page, who looked at him with contempt, and two other Halberdiers who looked at him not at all. He sat and waited there above an hour, and then he could hear voices through a tall doorway which led into the next room. One was high, a voice which when moved to anger, as it was now, produced a squawk much like a parrot inflamed, the other was soft, secret and reassuring, the voice of Master Secretary Cecil.

"By God's son, sir! You shall tell me. What said Robin before the actors?"

"I cannot speak it, my Lady. It would pain Your Majesty."

"Have I lived more than three score years with scheming Secretaries and not been pained? Come, if I can meet Spain's ships I can meet Robin Essex's words. What said he?"

Straining his ears Shakespeare could only just hear the answer he dreaded.

"He said, in the hearing of the actors, that your Majesty's bargains were as crooked as your carcass."

There was a long silence, and then the Queen's voice sounded quiet and dangerous. "You may prepare the warrant, Master Secretary." Then she called louder, "By God's son, ladies, where is the music? Are we all to be doused in melancholy!"

At that came a tinkling tune on some virginals, the door opened and Master Secretary Cecil came quickly out. Another ten minutes and Will Shakespeare, wishing he had never left Stratford or put pen to paper, was called in by a steward and knelt before Her Majesty.

\*     \*     \*

He remembered sunlight, streaming in from a high window, a dead white face in a scarlet wig, and a white satin dress like a bride's dress sparkling with jewels, glittering like the sun. Somewhere, he supposed, there were ladies; one stopped playing as he knelt in all humility. And then that voice came at him, now flicking him like a fire, now cold as ice, now gentle as a lover's voice, now terrible as the rebuke of a Prince.

"Master Shakespeare. What a little poet you are." Truly on his knees he was of no great height. "What a little, little poet. Oh, do stand, I pray you. Add a little to your stature."

"I ask pardon, Highness." Shakespeare rose awkwardly and stood abashed.

"Pardon? Why should I pardon you?" She seemed near to laughter. However, Will Shakespeare started to recite that cunning speech he had prepared during his long time waiting.

"We are but actors, but poor players. Shadows. Our masters call the tune and we must dance to it. We never thought to offend. What we did was done in simple faith and honest ignorance."

At which Her Majesty stifled a yawn. "Have you done? Such a speech would send your groundlings fast asleep." The ladies, who seemed young and pretty and were known as the Queen's Glories, giggled in the corners: which did not comfort Shakespeare, who looked helpless.

"Lost for words, little poet? Tell me, what is the great crime for which you seek my mercy? A halting verse? A limp rhyme to end a scene, as I have heard many times in your comedies."

"I had thought I had displeased Your Highness' Council."

"So you thought of my Council? You shadows trouble your minds sometimes then, with matters politic? How have you displeased my Council, Shadow?"

"There was the matter of the performance."

"The performance?" Her Majesty seemed not to understand.

"My Second Richard."

At which the Queen frowned and began to tax him like a pedagogue with a dull scholar who has spoiled a set of verses. "Your Second Richard! A poor play! Journeyman's work. Sorely botched. And I speak as one who loves playmaking,

and as one who studies History. I tell you, Master Shakespeare, you are in the wrong. There was no deposition!"

"No, Majesty." If she had said so he would have agreed
there was no flood, no nor Crucifixion either.

"No deposition! There was none, nor ever shall be. What
passed, passed by Inheritance and the Rule of Law. There
was no snatching of crowns. Hear that, little poet?"

"Yes, Majesty." The scholar seemed apt to learn.

"Improve your work in future. I have no time to teach you
History before each play you blunder into."

"I am grateful for Your Majesty's interest."

The Queen nodded and then gave a short laugh which had,
for the first time, a chuckle of humour in it. "I wonder, Master
Shakespeare," she said, "by God's son, I wonder, how a man
who could write me such a character as Fat Falstaff could so
botch the Second Richard?"

"All poets may fail, on occasion."

"True. But you are one who may stumble into a good
invention, from time to time. To redeem your poor standing
with me, sir, you may do something to purge my melancholy.
I know not why, it seems a sad season with us all. The stars
are in a crooked pattern, we are full of rash quarrels and it
seems, lovers fall out also. So let me have a good play, one
I did take much delight in, when old fat Falstaff and the
doddering Judge went out to pick an army. Come, will you do
that over for me?"

"We are to play here, at Court?" Will Shakespeare could
scarce understand it. He came expecting a scaffold and was
given a stage.

"And fill a Prince's hours with such smiles as your humble
quill may provide. You may go now."

As you may imagine he bowed very low and backed away.

He was nearly to the door when she called after him:

"Tonight you may learn how we manage our kingdom,
without the help of actors!"

# 32

## *Of How The Earl Of Essex Quoted Shakespeare*

I HAD NEVER been in a Palace before and wondered at the Miracle of playmaking that it could bring a boy from the hedgerows and actors' carts, who had no decent breeches when he was a child, to the Great Hall at Nonesuch, where the firelight and candles shone on polished marble and fine brocade, where the women's bosoms and the gentlemen's fine silks and velvets would send the senses swooning, and where only the dogs of the finest breeds pissed against the great hunting tapestry or under the ladies' footstools. There was music playing sweetly in a gallery, and on a platform lit with a hundred candles we gave Her Majesty what she had asked for, old Fat Falstaff, played by Dick Burbage with a belly strapped onto his own growing pot, in that fine chronicle of Harry the Four where Harry of England, like Hal of Southampton who that night lay in the Tower waiting his death, mixed with low company and foisted purses and tumbled pot-girls.

In the second part of that play, to which we came by judicious shortening for a Royal Occasion, I did enact Doll Tearsheet, something below my usual birth but a woman that was used to raise gusts of laughter from the groundlings but by her appearance. But that night there was no laughter. Our jests might have fallen on deaf ears, and our finest sallies brought forth nothing but silence. This dashed all our spirits, but we thought this was the difference between a Theatre and a Palace, till we learned that our noble audience knew that a decision was taken which might be put, at any moment, into action concerning him who had been that Court's favourite and had been certainly beloved in secret of all its ladies including the great Queen herself, who sat high up on a gold chair, stiffened, brocaded, ringed and jewelled, painted white and red, who never smiled once at all the merry humours of that Fat Falstaff she said she loved so well.

We came to that scene which I thought none can help but laugh at, when Falstaff and old Justice Shallow go to raise recruits for the King's army. Falstaff, played as I said by Burbage, and the old judge, to which Shakespeare gave a doting imitation of how Mr. Justice Fleminge might be in extreme old age, fingered through their memories before the sorry line of yokels standing to be selected for service.

"O, Sir John, do you remember since we lay all night in the windmill in St. George's field?" piped Shakespeare-Shallow.

"No more of that, good Master Shallow, no more of that," Burbage-Falstaff rumbled.

"Ha, 'twas a merry night. And is Jane Nightwork alive?"

"She lives, Master Shallow."

"She could never away with me."

"Never, never, she would always say she could not abide Master Shallow."

"By the mass, I could anger her to the heart! She was then a bona-roba. Doth she hold her own well?"

"Old. Old, Master Shallow!"

"Nay, she must be old; she cannot choose but be old; certain she's old; and had Robin Nightwork by old Nightwork before I came to Clement's Inn."

"That's fifty-five year ago." I was doubling the part of Silence in an old hat and gown and there piped up.

"Ha, cousin Silence, that thou hadst seen that this knight and I have seen — Ha, Sir John, said I well?"

"We have heard the chimes at midnight, Master Shallow!" Burbage said and then we all realised that no one in the audience was paying him the slightest attention. All eyes were on Master Secretary Cecil, who came to the Queen followed by a big man with ginger hair who carried a writing desk on which lay quill, ink and a long paper. Seeing this, the Queen interrupted our playing in a voice soft as a battle cry, or the Last Great Trump of Angels.

"Very well, Master Secretary. I will sign now for Lord Essex's present death. This time is most convenient. Let me have the paper. And bid the actors continue ..."

So we continued, while the whole audience looked at her and a few harsh scratchings of her pen ended the life and glorious career of Robert Devereux, Earl of Essex.

"Shall he die according to his sentence?" Cecil said as he took the paper from her.

That night, softened by Falstaff perhaps, the Queen was in a gentle mood. "No, Master Secretary. Let him be given the mercy of the axe."

On our poor platform we tried to stumble through that scene where the yokels beg and bribe their way out of the King's Service, and by liberal payments to Corporal Bardolph escape the call of the Army. We played through to dreadful silence and at last Hemminge spoke as Feeble, that spavined, knock-kneed, useless clod of a country bumpkin who yet has no wish to avoid his fate and will not bribe Bardolph but says he will go with him to fight the French.

"By my troth, I care not; a man can but die once; we owe God a death." So said Shakespeare's Feeble.

\* \* \*

"By my troth, I care not; a man can die but once; we owe God a death." So, in direct quotation, said the Earl of Essex as he stood upon the stage that had been built just for him. The page Hercules watched from a window in the Tower together with his master Southampton whose turn might come at any time. I pictured the Earl, shivering before the block, but still forcing himself to perform, like an actor will though death be staring him in the face. Robin Essex made several other speeches, the sense of which Hercules cannot now remember, and they were not writ by Will Shakespeare.

Then he took off his cloak and ruff and knelt to pray. At last he took off his black doublet, showing he wore a scarlet waistcoat with long sleeves. He told the headsman, who knelt for forgiveness, that he would be ready when he stretched out his arms. He lay low across the block, his long hair spread out, and then the scarlet arms reached forward as though to grasp some object unobtainable as the axe, sharpened at some expense, fell.

Hercules says his master was pale as paper for many weeks after and spoke little. That day I was the young lady Viola and, our troubles being over, thought only of our play, which finished as Armin sang,

> "A great while ago the world began
> With a hey, ho, the wind and the rain
> But that's all one, our play is done,
> And we'll strive to please you every day."

Business was good that day. Many had been turned away from the Tower, where the execution was, by the Queen's particular mercy, held in private.

# Part Six

## "THE LIVING RECORD"

"Not marble, nor the gilded
  monuments
Of princes, shall outlive this
  powerful rhymt.
But you shall shine more bright
  in these contents
Than unswept stone, besmear'd
  with sluttish time.
When wasteful war shall statues
  overturn,
And broils root out the work of
  masonry,
Nor Mars his sword nor war's
  quick fire shall burn
The living record of your memory."
                              Sonnet 55

# 33

## *Of How Shakespeare's Sonnets Were Demanded Of Him By A Gentleman In Black Garments*

WHEN SHAKESPEARE WROTE his Melancholy History of Hamlet Prince of Denmark the town was so taken with it that they say the tailors were quite out of black cloth. Many young gallants pictured themselves as that poetic and brooding Prince and strutted silent in an inky cloak uttering occasional strange thoughts about the patterns in the sky, or cursing their unhappy Destiny that ever they were born into a fine Castle or a Palace where lesser mortals drank beer and engaged in unnecessary jollity.

One man who had no doubt real cause for mourning dressed, in particular, most like Hamlet the Dane. Hercules told me that their lodgings in the Tower were none too comfortable, some of the diamond panes in the window were cracked, the straw he slept on was damp from the river and his master complained that the beds kept for the nobility in the Tower were not so soft as those at Titchfield. All the same they were able to bring in their own silver and table linen, victuals of good quality were supplied (though Hercules suspected the plovers' eggs were laid by the Ravens) and they had a good quantity of white Bavarian laid down in the cool of an empty dungeon. There were books for his master to read and a black cat to eat the rats and act as company. For all this Hal was in a fit of undoubted despair for the acting of which he wore a suit of black velvets, a black cloak, black gloves with white lace cuffs decorated with black love knots;

so with his hair long, his face pale and his smile sadly ironic
Hal, still alive near two years after his Hero gave his last
performance (owing that weak grasp on the world mainly to
the Old Queen's prevarication and hatred of decision), looked
a very Hamlet, a mirror image of the Prince of Melancholy.

And as black-clad Burbage stood on the Globe's stage
fingering his dagger, wondering if he might his quietus make
with that bare bodkin, so Hal in his lodging in the Tower
snatched a knife off the table where Hercules had laid dinner
and, pulling aside his shirt, seemed about to "not be" in
earnest when Will Shakespeare, his visitor and guest in those
gloomy surroundings, grabbed at his wrist and sought to
wrestle the knife away from him as Hal protested, "I'll cheat
Her Fatal Majesty, and the crowd of sweating citizens that
would make my execution a Sunday spectacle, like Bear-
Baiting!"

"Wait! My Lord Impatient!" Shakespeare twisted Hal's
wrist, in a sudden desperation to keep his friend alive, and
the knife clattered to the floor, where Hercules quickly re-
trieved it and returned it to its place by the cold pheasants.
Hal looked at Shakespeare and smiled suddenly.

"Is it mortal sin? Do you think that, Will? Has God no
more mercy than our cold Queen?"

"She may have mercy," Shakespeare comforted him. "I am
summoned to the court at Richmond. I have a word from the
Lord Great Chamberlain."

"Her Majesty wants a play?"

"No doubt. But I can tell her of your true repentance, Hal."

"She cares not a fig for my true repentance! She wants a
play! With Harry Southampton in a black doublet as the
principal actor!"

There had been a sound of hammering in the court below
which Shakespeare had tried to ignore, as he had avoided
looking at the wooden stage certain carpenters were erecting
beneath the grimy, diamond-paned window.

"I will play it without words." Hal went to the window and
looked down. "On that scaffold they are building now, with

no other actors but Master Headsman and no properties but
a keen blade, ground in France. And when I kneel to the
applause, God knows I shall not rise again." Hal turned from
the window to Will Shakespeare with a sudden urgent request. "Do you keep my immortality sharp? I shall soon have
a use for it. What did you write for me?" He seemed then to
remember it with pleasure.

> "Not marble, nor the gilded monuments
>     Of princes, shall outlive this powerful rhyme . . ."

"Is that true, Will?"

> "Nor Mars his sword nor war's quick fire shall burn
>     The living record of your memory,"

Shakespeare assured him.

> "So, till the judgment that yourself arise . . ."

Hal was frowning, trying to recall the line.

> "You live in this and dwell in lovers' eyes."

Will told him with certainty.

"Lovers?" Hal seemed altogether pleased. "I shall live as
a lover to the Day of Judgment?"

"Talk not of the Day of Judgment. By Spring you shall be
chasing the deer at Titchfield."

Hal shook his head, not to be persuaded, and said, "How
will they remember me then, from your verses?"

"Why, as one who was a true friend."

"Or as the friend to a true poet?" Hal seemed, on a sudden,
to suspect his friend. He burst out again, "Two years! Queen
Cat has played with me like a mouse! And now they prepare
a scaffold. Bring me my poems, Will. Bring them to me in the
Tower, so I may read my monuments. You keep them safe?"

"Of course," Shakespeare reassured him. "Safe in a coffer

at my lodgings." As he said this he had every good reason for thinking he spoke the truth, for this was the last place he had seen those sonnets wherein he spoke of his love for his Fair Friend and his Dark Lady.

# 34

## Of Word Pirates, And How Will Shakespeare Lost His Sonnets

I HAVE TOLD you that as Hal-Hamlet stood black-suited in the Tower fingering a blade and contemplating self-slaughter, Burbage-Hamlet stood on the stage of the Globe playing the same part. In our audience there lurked a kind of verbal vulture, a snapper-up of undelivered speeches, a very magpie of the Theatre, in the person of a certain unlicensed Printer who kept his Pirate Press in the neighbourhood of St. Botolph's alley and who was named Peter Filp. Now this Filp printed plays without a by-your-leave from their author or a penny to him, and having no access to written parts did his best to catch the words on the wing, as it were, and dictate them to his man Venus, who tried his best to jot them down on such scraps of paper as he had about him before the actors spied what was happening and kicked them both out of the Theatre.

Filp, a thin, scrawny bird of a person with greasy black hair and a threadbare jacket, his thin fingers stained with printer's ink, was hard of hearing, and his man Venus slow of scribble, so God knows what a shambles they made of any play they were set on transcribing. Matters went thus, as I learnt from those who stood near them and marvelled at their proceedings.

Burbage-Hamlet (from the stage):
    To be, or not to be: that is the question:

Whether 'tis nobler in the mind to suffer
The slings and arrows of outrageous fortune ...
Filp (yelling to Venus):
To be or not to live
That is the vital issue
Whether 'tis nobler in the mind ...
Venus (hand cupping ear): Blind?
Filp: No fool, mind!
Burbage-Hamlet:
Or to take arms against a sea of troubles,
And by opposing end them?
Filp:
Or to combat the mass of troubles ...
Venus: Mess?
Filp: That'll do. And by contesting, end them.

So you may see what a bastard by-blow of a play would be struck off Master Filp's press for the mouthing in Inn yards and ale houses so that it sounded, to rustic audiences, less like the work of William Shakespeare than a drunken Fleming cursing in Italian.

Having been booted quite from our theatre by Hemminge, Condell or ever sharp-toed Jack Rice if any caught him at his transcribing, the thieving Filp thought well to capture some real writing of Will Shakespeare, so he found out his lodging on the Surrey Bankside and hammered on the door and was admitted by Shakespeare's fat and homely landlady, one Mistress Dainty who, seemingly impressed by the human scarecrow before her, admitted him into the Poet's study where he stood surveying the Poet's possessions.

"This is Master Shakespeare's lodging?" crowed Filp quite overcome with admiration. "He writes here? At this table? This is the very Temple of his imagination? This is the furnace of his brain?"

"Does he owe you money?" Mistress Dainty found this visitor hard to fathom.

"He owes me nothing! I have the honour to serve him."

"Serve him? You have the look of those who serve writs

and summonses." Mistress Dainty had some experience, as a landlady of actors.

"Misleading, Madam! I deal with poetry, not with the law. And I am sent by Master Shakespeare from the theatre to bring his writings to him. He has writings about the room, no doubt," said Filp hopefully. "Children of his imaginings, sleeping peacefully, in these cupboards." He opened a cupboard door quickly, as if expecting twenty hidden tragedies to leap out at him.

Mistress Dainty told him, "He keeps no writings here. All his parts he brings up to the theatre, to the actors."

"And what then? When the play is done? Are they not kept here for Posterity?"

"The actors use them, I suppose. For wrapping fish." Mistress Dainty frowned, "Who is this gentleman, Posterity?"

"There are no pages here? No words at all?" The black feathers of the bird Filp seemed to droop in disappointment.

"I see some in this box. Might be laundry lists for all I know. I'm no scholar." At which Mistress Dainty opened a brass casket on the table and handed Filp a handful of papers, which were none other than Will Shakespeare's Sonnets entire.

Filp took them eagerly and started to read.

"Two loves have I of comfort and despair
    Which like two spirits do suggest me still
    The better angel is a man right fair
    The worse spirit a woman coloured ill . . ."

Filp looked up from the paper like an early blackbird with a succulent worm. "Why, Madam," he said, "this is a Sonnet."

Mistress Dainty said, "Is it now? I don't know about that. I see it's not a bundle of firewood."

"This must be what I am sent for. I will take it to Master Shakespeare, toot de sweet! In the flutter of an eye-lid! My master shall have what he wants!"

At which he rewarded Mistress Dainty with a silver coin, which the good landlady looked at in her hand. "Is it worth

that to Master Shakespeare?" she marvelled. "A silver sixpence for the fetching of a Sonnet!"

When Shakespeare came home and found that precious
casket empty he shouted at his landlady in a rage incredulous.
"You gave my poems away?" Those poems, which had cost
him so much living. *To a man who asked for them!*" He had
no time to say more, having to ready himself for a visit to
his Greatest Patron and Sovereign Lady, the old Queen in
her Palace at Richmond.

\*　　\*　　\*

The Royal Virgin had now almost reached the years I have
now attained, her skin was drawn so tight and her pale face
had the appearance of a skull, rouged and decked out with
a red wig. She moved slowly, her legs were tired and she was
worn out by the cares of State. I am worn out also, by the
cares of keeping the steps scrubbed, the graveyard tidy, the
brass polished, a scrap of meat in my belly and a sane head
in the midst of all these crazed Puritans. I have not even to
rule one small county and I go to bed with my back near
broke and my legs aching; so what a burden did She have
with all England, Spain and the Irish rebels to trouble her.
But Will Shakespeare told me her old eye was still bright
and restless as a sparrow hawk's, and she still spoke clear and
commanding.

He was taken to her in a long gallery and she moved towards him on the arm of Master Secretary Cecil. Ranged all
along the gallery like statues were the black figures of her
young Courtiers, all suited darkly, as if in mourning for their
lost youth, and the poisoned Royalty of Denmark. This was
the first cause of the Queen's complaint to Shakespeare.

"We do not love your hero in the black clothes, Master
Shakespeare."

At which Shakespeare, whose mind dwelt only on his dark-
clad friend, Hal Southampton, protested. "He was misled,
by firm and subtle companions and he in the dizzy drunken-
ness of youth."

"Besides which, he has corrupted all my Court!" She looked round with disgust at all the black shadows, who bowed low to her. "Truly I may die tomorrow, since all the young men of my acquaintance are ready dressed in inky cloaks to furnish out my funeral!"

"If I might humbly beseech Your Majesty's mercy."

"No, Master Shakespeare. Kill that moping Danish Prince of yours. We will hear no more of Hamlet!"

"Hamlet?" He was relieved that this immediate sentence was not passed on his friend. "My Hamlet? My Lady, I spoke of my Lord Southampton."

The Queen looked at him, and then put an old hand on his arm. "Walk with me to the window, where I can see you clear. Your arm, Master Poet. My legs are no longer obedient subjects."

So he moved with her, greatly honoured, to the embrasure of a tall window where, a little away from Master Secretary and all her attendant Hamlets, the Queen listened whilst the Poet did his best to plead. "True Highness," he started hopefully. "My Lord of Essex was to blame. He filled my young friend full of fancies, saying Your Majesty had enemies that would destroy her. So he came armed into the street."

But this talk was not to the Queen's liking. "Will you still prattle of your Lord Southampton?" she asked, impatient.

"Still of my friend, who helped me do that work which may have pleased Your Majesty."

The Queen was watching him, and when she spoke now it was so quiet he had to strain to hear her. "You are no Courtier! No, nor Lawyer either to plead his guilty client out of a hangman's noose. You do it badly and it ill becomes you. You and I. The light is dim. Is it all these black suits about us? You and I, a woman and a poet, why, we are giants, sir! Above all bowing Lawyers and scraping Courtiers. Soon, you will have no woman for your Prince."

"Majesty?" He was puzzled, with no hint of what she was about to tell him.

"Soon there will be standing here my cousin James from Scotland. He will make but a small King, full of fears and

nightmares. This is no hour, sir, for you to give us Dansker
Princes, brainsick of melancholy! Give us old fat Falstaff
again. Is there to be no more laughter in England?"

"Majesty, I devoutly hope so." Shakespeare felt they had
got far from the life or death of Hal.

"You hope so! Then set about your proper work. Get from
my Court and take up ink and paper! Master Secretary!" Her
voice rose to that parrot call again, and hunchback Cecil came
towards her, took her arm and they started to move away.

Shakespeare, who felt he was fast losing all hope of his
friend's life, followed a step to say, "And for the other
matter?"

"Other matter? What other matter?" The Queen paused,
looked at him, puzzled.

"What I had to say to Your Majesty, on the part of my
young Lord Southampton."

There was a silence, and when Her Old Virgin Majesty
spoke again it was with withering contempt. "Your young
Lord of Southampton would have us know he does not care
to die?"

"He hopes to live."

"Tell him. Tell him so does his Queen. Dying's an unpleasant duty. But we must all perform it."

Shakespeare felt suddenly weary, knowing his cause was
lost. "Then there is no hope?"

"None for us all, born under God's strict sentence." She
moved away with Cecil into the shadows of the long gallery,
leaving Shakespeare where he stood. "Stand not so solemn!
Give us fat Falstaff. At least we may laugh whilst we await
our separate scaffolds!"

* * *

The next dinner Hercules set out in the Tower for Shakespeare was to be a sad occasion. Will crossed the Courtyard
not knowing how he could tell his friend of the Queen's
indifference. But no sooner had the Turnkey let him into

the little room than Hal grabbed his arm, seeming concerned with one matter only.

"Where are they?" he near shouted. "Where are my poems?"

"I spoke with the Queen. She may be merciful." Will answered carefully, not thinking it a time to speak of poetry.

"Lies! All lies! I want those Sonnets now! So I may have them burnt!"

Had the world turned over, or the night burst into broad daylight Shakespeare could not have been more astonished. "Burnt, Hal? They are your immortality!"

Hal looked at him, bitter. "Robin Essex is still a Hero. How will I be remembered? As the lover of women and poets? As a vain strumpet Lordling who courted your mistress for a jest? You want the poems for your own fame, Will. Let the Noble Rebellion be my only epitaph!" At which Hal struck an attitude as near as possible like that of the Earl of Essex on the scaffold.

Shakespeare, who liked not this posturing in the face of death, said, "Hal. You are not yourself."

"Myself at last! And not the shadowy patron of a Great Poet which your verses made me."

"So, you would burn my work?" Shakespeare still could not believe it.

"Aye, I would!"

"Is that the truth?"

There was a silence and then Hal said, "Men don't lie so near the scaffold."

"Pray God you will live for another thousand verses. Else will life be a dull business for the rest of us."

"And when I die," Hal was full of bitterness, "would you have me a small carving on your Great Tomb for ever?"

There was much Will Shakespeare might have said, but his heart was too full of sadness, and anger, and pity, as Hal turned away his face. "Leave me now," Hal said. "You were good company for dinner. But a man goes best to a woman or death alone."

Having sported with a couple of women, and hoping for

someone to hold my hand when I lie dying, I do not know if this fine sounding phrase is altogether true. But Shakespeare took it as his dismissal.

"Good night then, Hal. When you come back to living you will like me and your poems again."

"Good night." Hal did not turn to him. "I hope you get a good price for them. Don't sell me for nothing, Will."

# 35

*Of A New Master, And A New Man*

THE QUEEN WAS sick, so sick that any other old lady would have been in her bed, if not halfway to her grave, but she would not surrender to this King Death any more than she would bow her knee to the King of Spain or any other Foreign Potentate. She stood, fully dressed and rouged, so they say, and whilst the pain racked her, her Glories and the Doctor had cushions brought so that if she fell at least she might fall softly. They say that when Cecil told her she must lie down she looked at him with that glittering eye and rebuked him saying, "Must is not a word you use to Princes."

So Master Secretary Cecil, seeing he could effect nothing with Her Majesty, wrapped himself in his thickest cloak and braved the misty air of the Tower to call on a black-clad gentleman under present sentence of death. Hercules saw the Turnkey admit him and then, waiting on his master, feigned sleep in a corner of their room, but listened carefully to what was said as he thought Master Secretary's Privy visit might be the first sign of hope since they had come to that Palace of Traitors. So he heard Hal tell Cecil that the Poet Shakespeare had gone to plead for him with the Queen.

"Put no trust in Poets, my Lord. You have a stronger ally."

"And who is that?" Hal looked at Cecil hopefully, Master Secretary being the most powerful ally a man might wish for, second only to the Queen.

"Why, time."

"I have little enough of that commodity!" Hal was disappointed.

"But perhaps enough. Soon Her Majesty's cousin James of Scotland will rule over us. His heart warms to brave young men." Cecil spoke awkwardly of a subject that came not easily to him. "Young men of courage and Manly Presence."

"What are you bringing me, Master Secretary, a sovereign or a bridegroom?" Hal smiled, a rare thing with him at that time.

Ignoring this, Cecil turned to the world of Politics. "The new King will have his favourites. As my Lord Essex's friend you may be the first among them. King James was ever warm in his love for my Lord of Essex and would have supported his . . . his adventure had he dared."

"If he wants me for his favourite, King James may have to dig me up and join my head with my body!" Hal got up and paced the room.

Cecil looked at him, and spoke very quiet. "Not if His New Majesty comes to us before Her Old Majesty has signed the warrant for your death."

"She has been an unconscionable time over that finality. Soon, I think, she'll call for a pen."

"In the way of God, she may be soon past calling for anything."

It took Hal some seconds to understand how hopeful that saying of Cecil's was. " *Soon?* Is she sick abed?"

"She is sick but swears she'll not lie abed for it."

Hercules remembers his master clenched his fists, as though the return of hope was a pain to him. "So we must race death, Her Old Majesty and I?" He looked at Cecil. "Why did you come to me?"

Without apology Cecil gave his most excellent reason. "Because I hope the new King's Favourite will remember the old Queen's Servants."

"So whoever wins the race, Master Secretary Cecil will not be the loser?"

Cecil answered nothing, but moved to the door. Hal shouted at Hercules to sound the bell for a gaoler. "Should the Queen be spared, by God's mercy and to the joy of all her realm," said loyal Cecil, "nothing must be said of what has passed between us."

"Courage. If I die I shall not betray you on the scaffold. And if I live, I shall be as politic as you, Master Secretary."

So the gaoler unlocked the door, and Master Secretary Cecil went home to spend the night writing letters, one being, undoubtedly, to that King James of Scotland who so warmed to brave young men.

\* \* \*

When the pain became too much for her, they say the old Queen put her thumb in her mouth to bottle up her screaming and still stood, with her eyes open like a horse four days and nights together. At last she surrendered and fell upon her cushions, causing by such a fall, as I remember it, a small tremor of the earth. The next morning the sun rose in a bloody mist, the cocks were silent and many of the beasts then pregnant miscarried. And after, well, as I recall, after, the Summers never seemed so hot, the Winters never so icy and sparkling, the ale was not so strong, the roses never smelled as sweet and the young girls' skin was not so clear, their bums not so well rounded and no one laughed as they were wont to do. Indeed you may count from that day the coming of the shadows which drew in when that tremulous King of Scotland first rode across the border, and grew darker in his son's time till by now, with the snarling Puritans Lording it over us, there is an eclipse of joy and total darkness over England.

It's an ill wind blows no one good, however, and the morning after the Queen's death Hercules awoke to the sound of hammering in the courtyard of the Tower. They were taking down the scaffold. When Shakespeare came to see his friend, he found Hercules directing certain gaolers in the packing up of Southampton's property on to a cart for its removal from that gloomy lodging.

"We are moved, sir, to a more spacious lodging," said

H

Hercules. "Truly the rat-hunting season is over and we ride for Royal Game now."

An obsequious gaoler staggered up from the dungeons with a basket of bottles which Hercules inspected. "Ah! The Bavarian white! His Lordship told me, 'If Master Shakespeare calls on me' . . ." He held up a bottle and looked at it suspiciously. "The tide's gone down in this one, Turnkey!"

"*If* I call. He dreams I would not call?" True they had parted badly the last time, but sure that was not for ever.

" 'Bid the Poet trouble himself no more,' my master told me. For the short of it is he has ridden North to meet his new master."

"His new Master?"

Hercules smiled, feeling greatly superior to this simple Poet so behind with the news. "Why, the new King, of course. We are no longer rebels. We are the King's men now!"

At which a gaoler came up with an arm full of black clothing, very Hamlet suits. Hercules gave the man the wave magnificent. "You may share those black attires among you. My Lord has ridden forth in silver and gold lace!"

*       *       *

From then the sun shone bright on the page Hercules, and a short month later there he was, as he clearly remembers, resplendent in a new livery of the Southampton colours, stood against the wall of the King's palace at Richmond, watching as his master knelt on a cushion whilst the new Scottish King, much prompted by Master Secretary Cecil, hung about his new favourite's neck the collar of the Garter, and seemed to take longer than was strictly necessary arranging it about the Earl to his satisfaction.

"My Lord Southampton, with your Earldom restored in the Peerage of England . . ." Cecil whispered.

"My Lord Southampton, with your Earldom restored in the Peerage of England . . ." King James repeated in a kind of Pictish accent nigh incomprehensible to any that inhabit civilised regions.

"We do create thee ..." Cecil led him.

"We do create thee," James followed.

"Knight of the most noble Order of the Garter." Cecil said it, but got no echo. James was busy reading the inscription on the garter badge.

" 'Evil be to him who thinks evil.' Is it not a good motto?"

"Your Majesty honours me, far beyond my poor deserving." Hal, who had long expected another sort of Royal attention to his neck, now sounded as cheerful as if he had never been in peril.

"The rewards of a noble youth. As I look at you. Stand! You may stand up now." Hal rose and James seemed delighted with his new stature. "Why there, you grow so tall in England! It must be the rain. As I look at you I see the very pattern of a noble knight!"

James now moved about the room and, from his ramrod position by the wall, the young Hercules marvelled at what a strange sea-creature had now come to rule over us in England. The King's head seemed ever too large for his body, his eyes were damp and his tongue lolled. As he spoke he could not control a dribble at the corner of his mouth (which they say was almost the only watering his face received, for he ever denied himself washing as Christians deny themselves meat in Lent). As he walked the room he for ever plunged his hand into his breeches to worry his codpiece (these same breeches being well padded behind so as to protect his rump, it seems, from sudden assault by assassins and their daggers). However, they say this King kept a sharp wit somewhere about him, and if you could tune your ear to the strange Pictish accent you might ever and anon, through the slobbering, hear a jest. Hardly, you might think, a figure to command respect of his subjects, but Hal, recently Gartered, stood before him as though before the wisest and most proper of Monarchs and, however the King looked and fiddled, betrayed no flicker of contempt. And in his turn the King looked on Hal with a kind of anxious doting.

"You'll no disappoint me, Harry?" he begged.

"Disappoint Your Majesty?"

"I have heard rumours, gossip about the Court." In his anxiety the King's hand delved deep in his breeches for consolation. "Gossip is vile, Harry! It is poison. I always listen to it!"

Wine was poured for the King and he drank it greedily, slopping a red rivulet down his chin. "There is tittle-tattle of your having dealings with an actor and his mistress! Dealings! Is that what you call it in England? Double dealings, we'd say our side of the border. Dark dealings, maybe. With the player and his doxy."

"Who has said so?" Hal was outraged, his hand went to his sword, a gesture which delighted the King.

"Aye, there's my young knight! My pearl of chivalry! Would you challenge him to single combat? Would you break a lance with him? No need for that! You might break your pretty neck into the bargain."

"Majesty, I must face him!"

"It was some lying rascal, no doubt. Thank God for lying rascals, Harry! We learn so much truth from them. Take a cup of wine now. England looks so much better, after a cup of French wine."

Hal allowed the King to hand him wine. "I trust Your Majesty has not believed these libels."

"I? I believe nothing. But I asked Master Secretary Cecil his opinion." The King looked at Cecil, who smiled discreetly and said nothing.

"And what did Master Secretary say?"

"I believe he said that any scandal now touching one so near the Throne, as you are, Harry, very near to my Throne, might greatly distress our Protestant allies in Europe." Master Secretary here bowed slightly to confirm his opinion and the King continued. "It would distress your father also, Harry."

"My father?"

"Why, an old foolish Scot who looks on you as a son, my boy."

"There shall be no breath of scandal."

The King nodded and taking a handful of sweetmeats from a silver tray held by a page began to urge them in the direction of his mouth. "As I rode into England," His Majesty told Hal, "the common people pressed about me. A crowd who could have done with a gallon of rose water poured over them." He looked at Cecil and muttered, "You told me to show myself to the people! What in God's name would you have me do? Pull down my breeches and show them my backside?"

Cecil did his best to smile politely and no one else showed themselves amazed at what a King they had here. Now chewing sweetmeats, His Majesty came close to Hal. "We're far better removed from that herd of gazers and pryers, Harry. And now, you are sworn of my Council and service, give them nothing that they may gawp and giggle at." He looked hard at his favourite. "There is nothing, is there?"

"Nothing. I swear it." Hal did not hesitate.

"No old secrets that may be tossed up in a lampoon or a bawdy ballad?"

"None."

So, much relieved, the King put a sugary hand on Hal's shoulder. "I believe you, my boy. My very perfect gentle knight."

\*     \*     \*

In his dark shop at the sign of the Turk's Head, in St. Botolph's alley, the thieving Filp and his man Venus were turning their creaking press in the printing of Will Shakespeare's Sonnets.

# 36

## *Of A Printing Which Brought A Great Embarrassment, And Of How A New Prince Hal Forgot An Old Friend*

In Stratford on Avon there was, as elsewhere, loyal rejoicing at the Coronation of James, that great and wise Christian Monarch. Citizens who had never seen him fiddle or dribble lit bonfires, danced Morrises, held fairs and drank rivers of bastard ale. There was a fair at Stratford and Judith Shakespeare, twin of the deceased Hamnet, now eighteen, was attracted to the tray of a pedlar. From him she bought ribbons, buttons, a love charm and a vilely-printed pamphlet to which she was attracted by reading on the front of it her father's name, and further interested by a notice saying it contained Sundry Sonnets of Love. So she took the pamphlet home.

Many years after, Hamnet Sadler remembered the explosion that then took place, and how he sat at the Shakespeares' table trying to calm his nerves with a cup of mulberry wine whilst Mistress Anne stalked the room in her outrage, and ever and again flourished the dreadful printing in his face.

"Two loves I have of comfort and despair . . ."

Anne was giving Hamnet a dramatic reading.

"Which like two spirits do suggest me still
The better angel is a *man* right fair!"

She paused, appalled at the confession.

"The worser spirit a *woman* coloured ill ..."

"My child Judith bought this off a pedlar!"

"Why, no man should have two loves, truly!" Hamnet was suitably shocked.

"If he had stopped at two! How many are there? A dark, dusky woman. Moorish? Do you think she's Moorish, Hamnet?" Having read so far Anne thought anything possible.

"Not Moorish, surely!" Hamnet was not exactly sure what being Moorish might imply.

"And a light gentleman. It makes me sick to read it!"

"Some painted player, surely, that apes a petticoat," said Hamnet with disgust.

"He has done some wickedness. Great wickedness, as do all those who haunt playhouses and bear-baits and bowling alleys."

"Aye, men will do wickedness, round the bowling alleys." Hamnet spoke from his knowledge of the world.

"But not to brag of it!" Anne released her rage. "Not to blast a trumpet and have it called out by the Town Crier to shame his wife and daughters! I could burn to death with this humiliation. To have it printed out in a broadsheet like a vulgar ballad. Who knows how much more of this Devil's handiwork may be a'printing? What then, will Master Parson read it? Or the Mayor and Aldermen? Or all our neighbours? What will Lady Lucy *think*?"

"We may get the printing stopped. We may complain to the Justices." Hamnet saw that some step must be taken.

"I'd be ashamed to have the Justices see this. What, Sir Thomas Lucy and old Squire Dawson, him who once stood my godfather, should I go and tell them I am betrayed for a Moorish doxie and an actor in petticoats?"

"We need a power! Some Great Lord who Will's afraid of, to make him keep this silent!" Hamnet had the first inkling of an inspiration.

"A man who could write this fears neither his God nor

his wife, nor any Great Lord either. Oh, Hamnet, Neighbour
Hamnet, why did he seek to wound us so?" Anne's rage
softened to tears.

"Danged if I know, neighbour Anne." Hamnet finished his
mulberry wine. "It's a mystery. Why, a man may sin; all men
do sin a little. But why, in the name of Lucifer, must they
needs write poetry about it?"

\*    \*    \*

Now I must intrude in this account of Shakespeare's difficulties the none the less sore and sorry troubles of me, Jack
Rice. Indeed from this time do I trace the start of that decline
in my fortunes which, continuing steady over so many years,
has brought me at last to a lonely old age in a draughty
vestry, with no comfort but these scribbled memories of my
past days of Glory. It may be said justly that my downfall
was due entirely to one thing, the Voice.

You must know that when I started this tale, at the time
when Hal Southampton was Hamleting in the Tower, and
Dick Burbage was playing much the same role on the stage,
I was an actress at the Zenith, the very peak of my perfection.
In short I was the fair Ophelia who, for love of the Prince and
grief at his stabbing of her father, runs mad and is thus given
a scene in Act the Four which for madness, grief and sweet
songs must break the heart of the stubbornest groundling
and lead him who plays it to fame everlasting. Well, I did
play the scene, which is a comfort to remember, but I played
it not long by reason of the Voice.

When I was a child I spoke as a child, and despite my
growing Roger I was able to talk and sing you gently as a
girl. Still when I had a beard growing strong to shave before
each performance I could give you your Viola, your fair
Rosalind, your learned Portia (the quality of mercy is not
strained, but is never to be found in the Theatre) and though
their voices might sink a little on occasion, as a maid's will
particularly when she be apeing a man, yet I could do well
as all these ladies  But, and I blame myself hugely, I did not

sufficiently pamper or preserve the Voice, for this Voice comes from the throat and into the throat I poured, in the days of my success, pell-mell Brandies, Wines, both of the white and the red, Bastard Ale in such profusion that the voice became roughened, became dark, became so soaked in strong liquors that, were it more musical, it could best be called basso profundo and at worst pickled.

I was not surprised when Dick Burbage, calling a special rehearsal, tried me again in Ophelia's song and no longer wondered why that deranged Lady had sounded like an old Sailor celebrating in a Wapping Tavern. By unhappy chance there arrived at the Theatre just then a youth of great beauty named Nathan Field. Once the friend (truly it was a sure way to success in the Theatre) of the playmaker Ben Jonson, Field had quarrelled with his patron and required us to set him to work immediately. My heart sank when Dick Burbage asked him to sing *my* song.

> "He is dead and gone lady
> He is dead and gone
> At his head a grass green turf
> At his heels a stone ..."

Nathan Field drank nothing but water with a little sugar in it. I cursed his guts and wished him a heavy dose of the Spanish fever, but he sang like a crazed girl bewildered by her grief. He took over Ophelia and lived on to play Cleopatra.

"Oh, Good Queen Rice," the bean-pole Alex Cooke could not resist saying as he heard that singing, "can it be your long reign is drawing to a close?" I was parted as Rosencrantz.

* * *

We were in the tiring room after *Hamlet* one day when Dick Burbage was called out to receive a letter. As we waited his return I sat miserable before the mirror and I have no shame to say I was weeping. Shakespeare crossed from his place and put his arm about me.

"What, real tears, Jack Rice?" He put a hand on my cheek and seemed amazed to find it wet. "Come, lad. Rosencrantz is not a weeping role."

"It's a role a man would weep to get if he has once played Ophelia."

"That's it! You are a man now. Time changes us all."

"I care for nothing but the ingratitude!" I told him.

"It's the nature of our trade, Jack."

"I, who have given them Lady Juliet and Queen Anne and fair Rosalind, now to be forgotten!"

"We are but shadows and ghosts, Jack, and shall all be forgot."

I looked at Shakespeare, thinking he but spoke to comfort me. "You forgot? You never believe it!"

At which there burst in on us, still in black clothes and carrying a letter, Dick Burbage, surely the merriest Hamlet the world has ever seen. "Where are my Hearts?" cried Burbage. "What? Long faces? Cold silences? Come, smile, Ghost. Come to your senses, the fair Ophelia. Open the wine barrel, King. Oh, this is a fair day for all."

Sam Crosse, King Claudius, went to tap the barrel. "Why is it a day for wine, Signor Melancholy?"

"Why? For we have a new King! And we are the King's Men now!" Burbage waved the letter. "His very favourite Privy Players. And we are each to have money to buy four yards of scarlet cloth for a livery to walk in his Royal Procession. And we are to go to Richmond Palace for our new Charter as the Royal Actors."

"Scarlet liveries! I have a young goat will march with us, to carry the drum!" Sam Crosse remembered.

"A Royal Charter! How will that be writ?" Hemminge was anxious the proper form should be observed.

Sam Crosse was handing out mugs of wine. "Did you say four yards for a livery?" he asked Burbage.

"Will that be enough to cover you, Burbage?" A sour note, but I could not resist it.

Burbage ignored me and went to Will Shakespeare, taking his hand and saying, "We are ever in your debt, Will."

"For my play?" Shakespeare was puzzled.

"Play? There be many plays. No, for your friend. Hal the Horse-thief climbed high in the King's favour, they say. Now you have a friend at Court, truly."

"Is that where he is?" Shakespeare turned to the mirror to wash the Ghost's paint off him. "Then perhaps I may find him again."

\* \* \*

So we dressed fine, all in our scarlet liveries, and went to Richmond Palace to receive our appointment and instructions, and were lined up in the Audience Chamber, where, on a far seat, the King ate sweetmeats and giggled to my Lord, the Earl of Southampton, who wore a golden suit and the ribbon of the Garter.

The Lord Chamberlain, who was once our patron, opened a scroll and read us our instructions. "You are the King's men now," he intoned. "This place brings you New Honours and New Responsibilities." I saw Will Shakespeare gazing at Hal, who being busy with His Majesty, never turned his head to him. Meanwhile on droned the Chamberlain, "You will give a play here at Court once each month and on certain Royal Feasts and Occasions, whereby you will be seen less by the Public in General as befits those players privy to the Court and Person of His Majesty. Attend there now." He went to the King and bent himself double. "Does Your Majesty wish to address His Players?"

"Address them? Heaven forbid!" we heard the King say, and then he turned to Hal. "Would you address them?"

"No, my lord." Hal was not looking at us.

"You may leave the presence," the Lord Chamberlain told us. "You will be served beef and small ale in the Lower Servants' Hall." Whereat he bowed, we bowed. We all began to move to the doorway, all except Will Shakespeare, who stood quite still, looking towards his old friend Hal who was moving to a door at the opposite end of the room, the King's hand on his arm.

"Hal!" Shakespeare spoke loudly and the King, amazed, turned to stare at him. Then he looked at his Gartered Earl and said,

"Do you know this player, my Lord Southampton?"

The King looked keenly at the Earl as though testing him. Shakespeare also looked at Hal, who shrugged, looked anywhere but at his friend and said, in a small voice, "I scarce remember, Your Majesty. I may have seen him act."

All we players were silent as groundlings at a terrible Last Act, and when the King's strange sing-song came to us, he was smiling at the Earl. "No harm in that, my boy," said James. "Come, we have business to discuss." And as he was moving with Hal to their private door he was offering him that which once belonged to the Earl of Essex, the monopoly of sweet wines.

Then, the Lord Great Chamberlain came to Shakespeare, saying, "Come your ways, sir. Will you go join the other players?"

They gave us much ale in the Lower Hall, and as much meat as you could skewer on your dagger. Will Shakespeare ate nothing.

# 37

## Of A Meeting At Oxford

HERCULES REMEMBERS A country fellow, a pink-faced, fair-haired man with big red hands come calling on his Master. This man was undoubtedly Hamnet Sadler. Later the Earl stormed down to Hercules holding a pamphlet, seeming to be a clutch of poetry.

"Printed by Master Peter Filp? At the sign of the Turk's Head in St. Botolph's alley. You will go there, Hercules!"

So Hercules went there with the tall footman and two other strong men in the Southampton livery. They took thick staves and a box of tinder. They knocked on the printer's door and the old crow opened to them.

"Master Filp, him that prints the poetry?" Hercules enquired politely.

"You are addressing no less a person!" Filp bowed and cackled.

"All right, lads," Hercules gave the command, "my Lord Southampton don't like poetry."

At which the Earl's servants smashed the press and set fire to all the printing they found there, in case they should contain those verses their Master once relied on for his immortality.

\* \* \*

Some time later Will Shakespeare was at the Theatre when

word was sent to him, by a man he knew not, that a certain
person wished to meet him urgently at the Tavern Wine Inn
at Oxford, which, as I have told you, was kept by Landlord
Davenant whose wife did certain favours in the past to
Shakespeare when he was a traveller, and who may have
given, all unexpectedly, birth to a Poet. Shakespeare, thinking it was some news of the child or other trouble with the
good Davenants, therefore agreed to be at the Inn in the
Cornmarket, Oxford, after dinner on a certain date.

It was dark and raining hard when he rode up to the Inn.
Landlord Davenant greeted him with a courtesy born of total
ignorance of how close Shakespeare was to being a member
of his family.

"You wish to see me?" Shakespeare looked puzzled at the
smiling Davenant.

"Not I, Master Shakespeare. They are all upstairs that wish
to see you, waiting in the private room."

Shakespeare went quickly up the stairs, puzzled as to
whom he should meet and perhaps hoping for some loving
lady, veiled and waiting for him. What he found, seated on
three chairs well spaced apart, unsmiling as three Judges
waiting to condemn him, were his friend the Earl of Southampton, his neighbour Hamnet Sadler and his wife Anne born
Hathaway. Surely never was so ill assorted a tribunal brought
together by night to accuse and judge a Poet.

*        *        *

"Anne!"

"I asked your wife to meet here privately so we might all
persuade you to stop this printing, Will." Hal, as Principal
Judge, opened the proceedings.

"This is what your daughter Judith bought of a pedlar!"
Anne produced the evidence.

"Think of your wife's fair name." Hal's voice was cold and
aloof.

Shakespeare ignored him and spoke only to his wife. "What,

Anne, are you come to warm yourself at this little Lordling's fire?"

"His Worship was all we thought to turn to, Will, to stop your foul rhymes a'printing." Hamnet was there to see Justice done, in the name of common sense and the decent folk of England. It was this reasonable voice which first made Shakespeare angry.

"Foul rhymes?" He turned on Hamnet. "Did you say *foul* rhymes?"

"Aye, rhymes of a foul lechery. That's what they be, surely." Hamnet saw no doubt about it.

"What is this dark woman, husband?" Anne asked, anxious still. "Is she Moorish?"

"*And* the fair gentleman with whom it seems you share your favours." Hamnet filled in the indictment.

"Your good wife's name is besmirched in the countryside!" Hal broke in, a little overhastily.

At which Shakespeare turned, slowly, contemptuously, and looked at his one-time friend as if for the first time, saying, "Who are you, sir? In good faith, I do not know you."

"How could I greet you at Court? I am close now to the King." Hal went on more quietly to Shakespeare, "I need no Poems of scandal and old adventures!"

Shakespeare looked round at his three Judges and addressed them all. "You need no Poems! None of you? Oh, they were welcome once!" He looked at Hal. "You called them your immortality!" And then to Anne. "And it was my words brought all that bright yellow money to Stratford that you kept locked away and dusted in a box. Words were welcome once, weren't they, my family? Now they must be strangled like a whore's child and hidden in a ditch; only because of the truth they tell about their birth. Have I lied once in these verses? Have I?" He looked at Hal, and then said wearily, "No, the lies were yours! When you would be a Dead Hero or a Living Courtier."

Now it was Anne's turn to rise and, pointing at Will Shakespeare, make good her accusation. "Have you done now, husband?" Her voice was low but strong when she was angry. "I call upon this Lord, this noble Lord, to hear me! I have stayed stuck at Stratford for nigh on twenty year. I have been shut off from all his light company and jesting actors, not to speak of such Dark Ladies as may engage his idle moments. Still I have worked and saved for him and kept the children clothed and decent without a father and expected no thanks. But how am I rewarded? With insults!"

"Insults!" Will Shakespeare found the charge unreasonable. "What insults? I have not writ a word about you."

"That's the insult!" Anne raged at him now. "So I may be laughed at for a woman whose husband writes of love to all the world but never to his wife!"

"Listen to the lady," said Hal graciously. "Your wife speaks but simple Justice."

"And you? Let's hear your simple Justice." Will rose once more to face his friend.

"That in this writing you show base ingratitude. To your wife there, and to me." Hal rose also, now it seemed the two men were arguing in a room alone.

"Ingratitude! Are you new-born without a memory? I have writ for your life. I have plead for your life. Not a gift I have but I have given it you, my Lord Ungrateful. And you have thrown each gift back in my face like slops from a window!"

"Your gifts! Your gifts are poison, little Poet. Your Poems are daggers and you lied in them."

"I lied!" Shakespeare was outraged, he may have lied in many places but surely never in a poem or a play.

"I read about the Fair Friend who should never be old. I read that I might last longer than rich marble or carved statues in the church at Titchfield. But then you betrayed me. You wrote of the Dark Lady and the Friend that did an act of darkness with her!" Hal seemed puzzled indeed. "Why did you write that, Will?"

"It was the truth. I needs must write it!"

Now Hal lost his judicial manner and showed his rage and his jealousy. "Needs must? Because they were *your* Poems, never *mine*. They were your Poems always. '*My* immortality!' You cared not a fig for *my* immortality. Not a snap of your fingers! I can die and be forgotten and the worms can eat me, so long as *you're* remembered. I swear to God! You shall not live for ever at my expense." He snatched the pamphlet from Anne. "I have had the Press broke that did disgorge these slanders!"

Shakespeare looked at him and unexpectedly smiled. "You did well, for once. The book's full of foul errors and gross alterations." He put his fist to his head. "I have the truth here. It shall never be destroyed!"

"It shall not be in print, I swear it!" Hal told him.

"Oh, but it shall; as it was writ, with every true syllable and rhyme intact. I have friends shall see to that."

"Friends!" Hal seemed not to believe it.

"I have no friends here but I have friends in my Theatre. In my Wooden 'O' are some that learn my words and love to remember them and live by their repetition. They shall have charge of a new printing. It shall be well done and carefully." Then Shakespeare, smiling again, gave Hal this consolation. "But courage, my Lord Terrified! No one shall know for sure they were your Poems. I will put a Cryptic Message in which you shall lie safe and hidden since it seems you fear words worse than axes. They shall be mine only. My Poems, my Immortality. And, as for you, my family, my wife.' He turned to Anne, and was no longer smiling.

"I could have sworn he had forgotten us," Anne complained to Hamnet, but her husband's next words froze her to silence.

"I had a son once died from your lack of loving," Shakespeare said. "My poems are my children, and you shall not kill them also!"

And so he walked out of the Taverne Inn. Outside, the wind had whipped to a fury, there was a roll of thunder and lightning lit the sky; and through that storm Shakespeare rode back to London.

# 38

## *Of This Great Stage Of Fools*

"Blow, winds, and crack your cheeks! Rage! Blow!
   You cataracts and hurricanoes, spout
   Till you have drench'd our steeples, drown'd the
      cocks . . ."

We were playing in the King's Palace at Whitehall, a long
warm chamber where the logs crackled in the fireplaces and
the brightest candles burnt, but on our platform there was
only darkness and storm and Dick Burbage, an old man
raging.

". . . And thou, all-shaking thunder,
   Strike flat the thick rotundity o' the world!
   Crack Nature's moulds, all germens spill at once,
   That make ingrateful man!"

Hal Southampton was sitting next to the King, who took
a sweetmeat from a gold box and seemed to feed it to him.
They whispered together and the King laughed.

Since the meeting at the Inn at Oxford, Shakespeare had
seemed changed to all of us. He sat remote, and often brooding, he acted no longer, indeed he had not done so since he
played in a most tedious play Historical by the playmaker
Ben Jonson which he had given before the Old Queen died.
When he spoke it was but to give us directions as to these

plays of Darkness, Death and Jealousy which he then made for us.

And what of those poems, those sonnets which Hal had wished burnt when he thought he would have to die, and had brought Will Shakespeare before his three Accusers in the Inn at Oxford? At first, when he came from that meeting he did nothing, writing at the two plays Tragical which then came into his head. But later he remembered all the poems and copied them again as he remembered them, leaving out nothing of his Fair Friend nor yet his Dark Lady. And when at last he had done this he gave the sheets to Hemminge and Condell who, ever business-like, found him a Licensed Printer of good repute, a certain Thomas Tusser, who had a shop and a press over against St. Paul's.

This done he set himself to a play so terrible in its railings against man's ingratitude that when given our parts we were half afraid to do it.

"What, dear Heart?" I recall Burbage saying. "Am I to do this at Court? I swear, my dear old friend, it will never, never please."

"To please," Shakespeare told him, "is not the play's intention."

I was parted as Oswald, a scoundrelly steward to one of the ungrateful Princesses in the play, and truly when I read the sheets over I could see so little good in the man that I thought how far had Will Shakespeare gone in his hatred of time-servers and double-dealers. It seemed he only saw a refuge from the world's ingratitude in madness, a state where Burbage Kinged it with a tattered dignity. When Dick started to say the words he could not resist them, and yet he was still afraid of how they might be taken at the Court.

The word in that play I heard most often was "ingratitude" and it came over like a bell tolling the last rites of the dead.

Behind our stage we shook the thunder sheet, blowing up a storm worse than any Shakespeare rode through from Oxford, and he stood, pale as I remember him, now with much of his front hairs gone and his forehead higher, peering through the curtain to where the jewelled courtiers sat, warm and made even more comfortable by the make-believe of our thunder, and where the squat King, ruler of all of us, jested with his favourite, Hal.

And on the stage Burbage-Lear told the blinded Hemminge-Gloucester of his views on Government. "Thou hast seen a farmer's dog bark at a beggar?"

"Ay, sir."

"And the creature run from the cur? There thou mayst see the great image of authority: a dog's obeyed in office."

At which the King was seen to smile with a deep satisfaction, and pop another sweetmeat into his mouth. He was still smiling as Burbage-Lear railed on at him.

> "Robes and furr'd gowns hide all. Plate sin with gold,
> And the strong lance of justice hurtless breaks;
> Arm it in rags, a pigmy's straw does pierce it."

With which Burbage, weary with so much indignation, turned on the blind Hemminge.

> "Get thee glass eyes;
> And, like a scurvy politician, seem
> To see the things thou dost not."

Seated next to the King, Southampton listened with great politeness and a small smile, now and then stealing a glance at the great clock above the fire, to see how long it would be to dinner.

On the stage old Lear held out his leg that they might pull off his boots.

> "... Now, now, now, now;
> Pull off my boots; harder, harder; so."

And weeping real tears now he looked at the pitiful, bloodstained face of Gloucester.

> "If thou wilt weep my fortunes, take my eyes.
> I know thee well enough; thy name is Gloucester:

Thou must be patient; we came crying hither:
Thou know'st, the first time that we smell the air,
We waul and cry. I will preach to thee: mark.

. . . . . .

When we are born, we cry that we are come
To this great stage of fools . . ."

At the end of the play the whole Court stood and clapped politely. They stood stiff in their fine clothes, like a row of dolls and we, the actors, bowed to them. Then they filed away, the King and the Earl leading, in strict order of precedence.

We started to dismantle the stage and pack away the properties. All of us, except Will Shakespeare, were jubilant at our good reception and thankful such a hard task as *Lear* was brought to an end.

"Well, that passed off well," said Sam Crosse.

"It passed off," Will admitted.

"I were sore afraid" – Sam Crosse spoke for all of us – "of all that railing at the Great Image of Authority! Of all that you wrote, Will, of Ingratitude and Scurvy Politicians! Well, I were feared the King and his Courtiers might take some offence at it."

"Were you so afraid? Were you all?" Will Shakespeare looked round at us, seeming surprised.

Burbage, restoring from a mug of wine some of the sweat he'd lost acting and chewing a duck's wing (he was ever hungry after a Tragedy) said, "I had some doubts also, Will, how it might be received. It is not well to berate Authority, not in a play. It never pleases."

"But to be sure they clapped and smiled at King Lear's mad railing as it were a Comedy!" Sam Crosse was delighted.

"So are we still the King's Men, and may get a new suit of scarlet cloth at Christmas!" Alex Cooke was, as ever, marvellously well pleased with himself.

Will Shakespeare turned on him. "And a warm blanket and a bundle of firewood and half a crown to drink His Majesty's Most Loyal Toast and a Health to that Great Lord Political,

Hal of Southampton, who in his better days was a Rogue and Vagabond like us."

"We are not rogues, Will!" Burbage was sitting, to refresh himself, in one of the courtier's chairs. A boy stood by with his well-brushed suit of velvets.

"No, not Vagabonds either." Sam Crosse thought of his small house and garden, his two warm cloaks and his milch cow and chickens.

"To them we shall always be Vagabonds!" Will Shakespeare answered him. "Why do they smile so when we rail? And the more we rail the more they smile at us! We show them their Ingratitude, their Hypocrisy, their short, strutting, empty Authority and Insolence in Office! And they smile and put their hands together and say, 'Thank you, actors, there is beef and small beer for you in the Lower Servants' Hall. And as there is no real offence in you, you shall have a suit of scarlets.'"

"What, would you have us give offence, Will?" Burbage asked reasonably.

Will stretched, like a man ready for sleep, and then I saw something I had not seen for many months; he was smiling. "No longer. There was a time for railing but it is over now. We have railed till the Heavens cracked and at least we feel the better for it. Now I must be silent a little. Now I must make amends."

"Now is the end of the world! Now is Will Shakespeare silent." I laughed at him, and he still smiled.

"Not the end of the world either, but a pause. I shall be gone now, for a little while."

"He's going into the country!" said Alex Cooke.

"With the Earl?" Burbage asked him.

"Earl? I know no Earl now. It seems I forgot where I came from. I must go find that place."

There was a long silence; then Burbage gave voice to all our thoughts. "You're never leaving us, Will?"

"For a little. I bid you all good night!" And then Shakespeare moved among us, taking a hand, resting his hand for a moment on a shoulder, bidding us all goodbye. "Dick, why, tonight you showed the King a true Monarch of Wrath and Madness. I never knew you could climb so high a mountain."

"It was a cold height," said Burbage. "Write us a comedy next, that I may laugh in the valley."

"Armin, my truthful, serious fool."

"I sang too low." Armin was worried. "The voice was drowned in the thunder."

"The voice was *non pareil*! Sam Crosse. How do you like acting in Palaces?"

"The food is good," said Sam. "But you can't keep hens in them."

We all laughed and then he bade goodbye to our men of business. "Condell, Hemminge, count the King's money. Don't let him cheat you." So he came to me. "And you, Jack Rice, I like you better now than when you were a girl!"

Something was ending, but I knew not what. But I thought we should be quite lost if he were leaving us. "Come back to us soon, Will. We cannot get a living without you."

He looked at us all. "Nor I without you. In my poor trade I have only one thing precious : your voices." Then he stepped from the platform and walked away, his steps echoing on the marble of the King's Great Hall at Whitehall Palace.

Hemminge called after him, "Go to Master Tusser's, Will. He has your poems ready for the printing."

Shakespeare didn't answer but walked on. When he was at the door Burbage called after him, "Will! Will Shakespeare!" But Shakespeare had gone and the door was closed after him.

\*     \*     \*

I heard later that he then went to Master Tusser where his poems were indeed ready for the printing. I had it off Hemminge, who had it off Master Tusser himself, that having been told that the print was set to reproduce his sonnets and keep them Immortal, Shakespeare paid the printer. Tusser then asked if he should start the press, but Shakespeare was moved to look at the rows of leaden letters.

"This is my print," he asked Tusser, "to do with as I please?"

"You've paid for it, sir. It's yours," Tusser told him.

"Thank you, Master Printer. By your leave. It seems, these poems would have done hurt to many." At which, taking up a mallet, Shakespeare struck away the type, the letters falling in a tinkling shower about the shop, like hailstones that may melt as soon as fallen. That done; he smiled and left the Printers.

# 39

## Of A Homecoming

DOCTOR JOHN HALL of Stratford, they told me when I visited that town, was a most ingenious and skilled physician. He was able to cure the collick with a beer brewed of watercress, brook lime and scurvy grass; true he relied something too much on cock's guts, spiders' webs and goats' excreta as sovereign for Melancholy, but he was a man of respected morals who inveighed against such as wore their hats in Church or put their hands there into ladies' skirts. So Doctor Hall was in all ways considered by Anne a most desirable suitor for her eldest daughter Susanna, who had grown to be a girl of wit and judgment, who could bake, sew embroidery and write her name with considerable ease.

So Doctor Hall went courting to New Place, Shakespeare's fine house in Stratford which had ten fireplaces, no less, and was the second biggest house in the town, no less, and had a garden of great vines and a mulberry tree; to such things may a man come but by staining paper with ink and using the mouths of actors.

So they were sat there, warm by one of their ten fireplaces, Anne at her sewing and Doctor Hall and Susanna playing a catch together on the recorders, and young Judith doing nothing much but roast chestnuts and wish she were courting also, when they heard the street door open and in came, quite unexpected, the Master of the House.

Judith ran to kiss her father and Anne looked up from the

fire. "What, are you back to Stratford?" She took up her needle again. "Are there no Dark London Ladies and Fair Gentlemen to entertain you?"

"No, truly, Anne. I have taken a wooden hammer and scattered them to tiny fragments. They are but a heap of letters on the floor of a printer's shop."

"You talk in riddles to make a fool of me. What do you want of us?" Anne sewed hard, making sure she showed no pleasure at his return.

"A mug of strong beer. It's been a cold journey." Judith ran to fetch it for him, and the young couple, having laid down their recorders, stood respectfully.

"This is Doctor John Hall," Anne told her husband, who was ever behindhand with news of his family, "who comes here to court Susanna."

"I would have asked you, sir, but you . . ."

"I know it," Shakespeare admitted. "As a father I am somewhat absent. So, little Johnny Hall. Are you a leech now?"

"It's as well to have one in the family with a learned profession!" Anne did not much care for this way of addressing the good Doctor.

"I thank you, Doctor Hall, that you should have turned your professional eye on my daughter. I only prescribe poetry. I am not learned enough for purges." Shakespeare bowed respectfully.

"Will you not bless us, sir?" Doctor Hall was a moderate man, determined to take no offence.

"Sure I will bless you. Did you wait for that before you took the long walk to Shottery?"

Judith then came in with a mug of beer. Shakespeare smiled at her and sat by the fire and drank in comfort. "We took that walk in the Spring, Father," Susanna told him. "We went to gather primroses."

"So did your mother and I. But we never stopped for primroses." He stretched out his legs, the warm logs drying his boots. "Anne, we should walk to Shottery tomorrow."

"It's Winter, bitter cold for walking." Anne's voice was softer and she sewed more slowly.

Shakespeare looked at her and spoke gently. "You may rest quiet now, Anne," he said. "The poems will not be printed."

"Good!" But she still made her protest. "Not that you can undo the dark deeds you wrote of so tenderly."

"The deeds are done. But I never wrote tenderly. I wrote as I felt, with terror sometimes." He rose and smiled at the young lovers who were now sat at the table, holding hands and gazing at each other. "I remember, Johnny Hall, you used to faint at the sight of blood. Now you are a Doctor! When shall you be married?"

"Next month," Anne answered for them. "I wonder you concern yourself so at our country doings. You who have verses, to make you immortal!"

And then Shakespeare turned to her, saying, as the good Doctor Hall remembered, "There will be no immortality! Players may speak my words, give them breath and then they vanish into the air! My words are lost and gone and that is best for them. And I shall be forgot also." They all looked at him, not understanding what made him so passionate. "Forgot!" he seemed to love the word. "Like the best actors and the best play when it is done; gone like shadows in the sunshine I tell you, I have come to tell you, good wife Anne, and now I can stay a while, men will remember the love-sick Doctor Hall and his pills and his potions at Stratford longer, much longer, than I shall be remembered. I would I could end now. With such a peace."

Now Anne had put down her sewing and truly smiled as he sat down with her again beside the fire. Later, bread was brought in, a strong cheese and cold cuts of beefs with more strong ales and the family ate supper together.

Shakespeare was not granted his wish, however. That night nothing ended, nor, like an old actor scribbling in a vestry, could he ever be forgot.

# 40

## *An Epilogue By Me, Jack Rice*

NOTHING IN OUR world being set fast as the stars in heaven, love ever turning to hate and then to love again, youth to old age and, in my sad case, young girls to old men, so no determination is ever fixed, and no decision for ever final. Four or five years later those selfsame Sonnets which had caused so much trouble and heartbreak were collected up, printed by one Master Thomas Thorpe and sold by John Wright at Christchurch Gate. I cannot say for sure if Will Shakespeare arranged their publication, for the printing was ill and the mistakes many; but the book was prefaced by an enigmatic dedication to a Mr. W.H. So, as had been promised, was the name of Mr. H.W., or Henry Wriothesley, disguised, and what had seemed to those concerned an event likely to crack the Heavens and bring about the Ending of the World, passed but as the sale of certain pleasing and well-turned verses, and the stories contained therein, being those tales of Love, Lust and Disloyalty, combined with the ever-present thirst for Immortality in the Poet and the Earl, passed but as the myth of a bygone age, which the writer may have drawn on or invented to provide his subject. Indeed so harmless and pleasing were the poems judged to be that Lady Lucy called on Mistress Shakespeare to tell her how much she had enjoyed her husband's Sonnets, and she would he wrote more in so gentle a vein. Lady Lucy swore she had read the tale of the

Fair friend and the Dark Lady before, in some book of old legends, translated out of the Italian.

Nor did Will Shakespeare spend, after that night I have described, all his nights in Stratford; but came often to London with a new play in his pocket, although he stayed no more at the Taverne at Oxford, but shunned the place, and Mistress Dainty wondered how she had offended him, and if he had found a new, and no doubt younger, way to break his journey.

Soon after Master Thorpe's bringing forth his Sonnets, however, Will began to rest almost solely at Stratford, being much concerned with his Tithes, his Barns, his Rents, his Rights of Way, the price of Grain and the pruning of his great vines. He was also greatly occupied with the composition of his Will, on which he spent, I have been told, more time than he did on the whole writing of *Hamlet*. In his writing of Prospero's Island he told of a magician who broke his staff of magic and drowned his book of spells deep into the sea. So to be sure did he live at the end as that retired Prospero, avoiding theatres and looking into books chiefly to write up there his accounts, or chronicle the crops grown in the fields of which he had bought an interest.

I do not think Shakespeare and Hal ever spoke again. Their friendship over, the Earl grew at last to full manhood, and in time shook off the damp hand of the King from his sleeve, and was able to oppose the Royal Wish when he felt it right to do so. He became much occupied with trade and plantations in the Americas and died, at the end, of a fever whilst on a visit to the Low Countries.

And what of me, what of Jack Rice? For a while I remained of the King's Players; but I never took well the loss of my petticoats. To have to play all day the man, with no two hours of being beautiful, light hearted, wanton and much desired, sent me into a melancholy, and the melancholy sent me to the bastard ale and thence to the stronger waters. I became not only Rough Voiced but Big Bellied also, and the more I grieved for my loss of womanhood the less likely I was to achieve it. One day, able to endure my deprivation

no longer, I persuaded that flute-voiced Nathan Field, who
was quite unaccustomed to strong drink, to come to the
Dagger Inn with me, and there I had him mixed such a potion
that he was quite overcome with it, and fell into a death-like
stupor at the time when the play was forward. At which I
ran back to the Theatre, contrived to come at his costume and
lurched on to the stage (for in tempting Nat Field I had
shared much of his potations) in the person of Queen Cleopatra. My joy at feeling the Royal Silks about my legs was
tempered by the drink I had taken and the fear of falling into
a swinish sleep on Egypt's throne. When the play was done
Dick Burbage called me to him. Ever kindly he hesitated to
dismiss me outright but told me that, in all conscience, he
could now only part me as attendants, or persons dead on
the battlefield. So I left him, comforting myself with the
thought that the King's Men had become so staid and respectable (Hemminge and Condell were now sidesmen and Parish
Councillors) that no joy or merriment was to be had in their
company. In my heart I was still angry, although I swear
I took no part in the burning down of the old Globe Theatre,
which was a matter purely accidental (although the Puritans
took it as a sign that Almighty God had at last come round
to their way of thinking).

I left to join a cry of players greatly inferior, who acted in
Inn yards and toured the country. I was given roles moderate
to minor; although I never aspired to womanhood again.

One Spring we stopped our actors' cart at Stratford (having
played the night before at Warwick Castle where the Lord
and his friends mocked and were pleased to throw bread at
us). We set up our platform in an Inn yard to give there the
old play of *Tamburlaine the Great*, for we had nothing new
to offer. I was parted as some minor king or chieftain and
when our stage was set and our properties disposed, I went
into the Inn to refresh myself before the performance.

"Hey there, player! You be one of the players no doubt?"
I was accosted by a local worthy, a man with a blue eye, grey
hair and comfortable paunch, none other than Hamnet Sadler,
who had come down with the good Doctor John Hall to

make sure that the wandering players made no attempt to call on, or otherwise disturb, that old wandering player Will Shakespeare. Mistress Anne Shakespeare had, it seemed, had troubles enough that month. Her younger daughter had married to a certain Quiney, who had been denounced for adulterous unchastity from the pulpit, and other domestic disasters had occurred, including the fact that old Ben Jonson and another poet had come visiting Shakespeare. He had joined them in a tavern and had so well recalled the old days, and had taken in so much ale in their recalling, that Master Shakespeare had fallen into a fever and must not leave the house. Truly, Hamnet told me, he was on the mend, thanks to Doctor Hall who had administered to him the windpipe of a cock ground into a fine powder; but he must hear of no players' visit nor any play forward, else he might be tempted out into the air and so delay his perfect recovery. I gave them my promise and in return they both saw "Great Tamburlaine" and after we sat a good four hours in the Inn together, during which the Poet's neighbour Sadler, and his son-in-law Doctor Hall, told me much of what is here set down, in these memories of times which shall never come again. "Tamburlaine the Great," sighed Hamnet Sadler, swaying like a tree in the wind as he left. "I mind how I brought Will a capon, and he lied to me, saying he played Tamburlaine the Great. He was ever a marvellous liar, was Will!" I last saw them arm in arm up the High Street, singing a catch, as drunk as actors.

We played for two days at Stratford, but most of those who had a taste for the play came on the first day, and on the second we played to but a sorry audience, who, in a windy scutter of rain, shivered on empty benches. That night I drank with our company, and it was very late and we were not still sober when we had the cart loaded. But next day we must play at another town so we whipped up the tired horses, rattled off down the empty streets, and I started to doze under the canvas of our cart.

It was as we passed a fine house with many windows that I thought I heard him. True, the wind was boisterous and the rain pelted down, but I thought I heard the voice of Will Shakespeare, calling to me to take him with us, for he had a mind to leave Stratford and go for a player again, as he had before, at the time of his beginning. No doubt I was dreaming, for when I opened my eyes the big house was still in darkness, and there was no sound but the wind flapping the branches in its great garden.

I heard that night he died. I think it was his birthday.